ROSEMARY T. MUPAMBWA

Exhume or Heal: A Widow's Memoir, Getting Her Groove Back

Authors Without Boundaries

First published by Authors Without Boundaries 2019

Copyright © 2019 by Rosemary T. Mupambwa

The contents of this book are not alternative for professional advice. The author doesn't present any advice given as a consultation and readers are adviced to seek professional help if required.

First edition

ISBN: 9781708628284

This book was professionally typeset on Reedsy.
Find out more at reedsy.com

Contents

Acknowledgements

I am grateful to the following people who have remained steadfast in supporting and encouraging me. These people have also pushed me to be the best I can be. They believe that I can change the world with what God has given me. They have helped me to reach this stage in my career:

First and foremost, my parents the late Mr Mathias Maponga and late Mrs Esther Maponga who were always pushing me to do my best in all my endeavors. Although you are not here to read this book and cheer me on, I know you are looking down on me and praying for me. I would have never written this book without the exceptional help and encouragement from my three children; Ruvimbo Natasha, Ronnie and Ropafadzo Tsitsi Mupambwa. You believed and encouraged me to write this book so it can help other women who have walked in the widowhood journey. My siblings: Mavis Mutanga, and Priscilla Chihota who helped to get the visa, and paperwork for my children processed. Patience Maponga Nyamupanda and Memory Ratidzo Bare. Abigail Maponga and the Late Tonderai Revson Maponga, thanks for looking after my children. Ivy and Willard Chiinze helped me with the USA visa application and looked after me when I arrived in the USA. Mercy Shambare connected me to her friend in South Africa. Lizzie Mabariki who picked up the paperwork for the Canadian Visa for my children. Without these people, I would not have been able to get my children to Canada. My children are the source of my strength.

Major Mrs. Mabhiza of the Salvation Army, was my prayer warrior when my husband passed away in 2000. The Salvation Army Brass Band and the whole congregation at Mbizo Corps, have been a huge spiritual support in my widowhood journey. I would also extend my gratitude to Mrs Janet Mashiri who has stood by my side to this day. Shannon Conner is a sister that I never had. She has believed in me and has always encouraged me and lifted me up when I was at rock bottom. My prayer warriors Madzimai Getrude and the members of the Johanne Masowe VeChishanu, Edmonton who have prayed and fasted with me. Mr and Mrs Ngoni Maenzanise and Aunty Memory Matanda who prayed with me when I started writing this book. Mr and Mrs Herbert Sinamano who have also prayed with me and encouraged me to continue doing my best in manifesting my gifts. Ms Josephine Mandizvidza has also prayed with me and encouraged me to write this book. My team at Elbow River Healing Lodge, my friends from AHS Liz, Laurel, Joanne, Nancy, Dianne and Shane. Blue Cloud and Scott for helping me with the proofreading.

To Gregg Michealssen, I would like to say thank you for giving me the pointers to write and self-publish this book. Monica Kunzekweguta and Jonathan Oladeji who did the editing and the publishing of this book.

Introduction

Widowhood sometimes feels like the job no one applies to. I am yet to meet anyone who has done this yet. This is what it means to be a widow, you wake up one day and your life has changed. It does not matter how your spouse died, you and the other women, you will be in the same category; widows. The husband might have died after a long or short illness, suicides, car accidents, plane crashes or heart attacks, it doesn't matter how it happened. It also does not matter whether your spouse was rich or poor. Sometimes people can call you a "rich widow," if your husband died and left you lots of money. This was a term used in my country, Zimbabwe, for widows who happened to inherit somewhat large benefits from their husbands. The fact remains the same. You have become a widow, and nothing will ever change that fact.

Going through widowhood or divorce can be a devastating life stage that will change the trajectory of your life after you marry the love of your life. No one is prepared for either widowhood or divorce when you say, "I do." You marry for love, forever and for a lifetime.

Sometimes that lifetime is cut short sooner than you expected. No one has a manual to life, neither are we given the manual for widowhood or divorcee. It is painful that people expect you to know how to behave or act like a widow.

This book while avoiding assumptions, is an attempt to guide you through life after widowhood or divorce. It will take you through some of the stages from the time you lose your spouse, to the funeral or separation, to the grieving process, and even covers some of the dumbest things people will say to widows.

It will also take you through the healing process. It shows you how self-love and transformation follow rediscovering who you are. The widow's journey is full of nasty surprises and mind-boggling life experiences. Re-inventing yourself through this book will prepare you to get your groove back and start a new life in the normal world from widowhood.

When you got married, you went for premarital counseling to prepare for marriage. When you suddenly find yourself a widow or divorcee, it's a new and different ball game. The widow must look for information to help herself through this phase. The pastor and family will scratch on the surface. There will be a lot of unanswered questions that pop up in the life of a widow.

You will ask yourself questions like, "Why does death happen to some marriages and yet some others have 60 years of married life?" You would wish anyone could give an answer to this. But, "***Dhololo.***" Nothing. When I got married, I remember saying to my husband, "Till death do us part," and him saying those same words back to me. I had no idea that those same words were going to haunt me twelve years later.

I have lived and walked this path that you are on. The paths we take might be different, but we still belong in the same pool, **widows.** I have lived with people whispering about me, or people pointing at me in any public places; stores, buses, train stations, hair salons, you name it. It was a hard and traumatic experience. It was like a nightmare. I hoped I would wake up one day and be told it was just a dream, but it was a real-life experience. It was like I had smeared a people repellent cream to chase people away from me. Some people will say some nasty things to you like, "you are faking the grieving process." Just walk away. Trying to explain the pain you are going through to the onlookers, is a waste of your time. Save that energy to Heal.

Let me tell you that life does not have to remain this way; gloomy, miserable, frustrating and lonely. This journey has made me the strong woman I am today. I believe strongly, I will be able to help a lot of women who are walking in the Widowhood Walk. After reading this book you will see that it's possible to come out as an even better person than you were before.

"You cannot be a victim and heal." (Picture quotes.com).

My late husband Temba, left me three beautiful children, two girls and one boy. At the time of his death, my eldest daughter, Rue, was only 12 years. My son, Ronnie, was nine years, and my youngest daughter, Ropa, was only five years old. Ropa, barely remembers her dad. It breaks my heart every time she tries to learn more about her dad.

The widowhood journey is tough and challenging. You can survive it, but it requires some work on your part as the widow. This book is written to inspire other women who might be going through what another widow went through so that they can learn from that experience. I hope that you know that you are not alone in this journey through this book. I came out stronger, so can you! You are not your problem, life does not happen to you, but you as the individual happens to life.

This book will show you, how I have lived the life of a widow. How I have dealt with having people point at me in the mall or grocery stores. There were those stares from people that either sought to shame me or felt sorry for me. Sometimes it's the *"poor her"* look. Other times it's, **"well she married the guy who is no more, so what?"** look. If you are a widow you will understand what I am talking about. It's normal to get those weird looks. You feel empty and feel like you are floating in the air because whatever was grounding you has been taken away from you. Just remember even if your husband is gone, there is another safety net that will always be there to catch you when you fall. That's is the God Almighty, whose love for you is unconditional. That is what kept me going, to this day.

When you are going through the pain, frustrations of the big void in your life, ask yourself, "How long do I have to go through this?" You learn to live with that pain. Help is out there, but it requires you to do most of the work. You are the only person who has the power to change your circumstances and the power lies within you. You are the captain of your ship and you can steer it whichever direction you want. I steered mine towards success and I did not let the struggles and challenges hold me back anymore. Don't let the past determine your future and the future of your children.

This book will teach you about the different stages of widowhood. You are likely to experience these three stages namely, grief, growth, and finally, transformation. During the grieving Stage, you are numb, and it's a vulnerable time for you. This is the time you need to be heard and understood, which usually never happens.

The growth stage is a critical part of your journey through widowhood. Now you start to take care of your business, your housing situation, finances and general planning for your life. The whole business with the estate for your husband should all be done by now.

The last stage is the transformational stage. This is when you do advanced planning for the new life to evolve. You are starting a new life and getting your independence from the bondage of widowhood or divorce. You might ask me why this is. It's because you are going through the same grieving stages of a relationship that is no more. You are no longer married, neither are you a couple with the person who was once the love of your life! Of course, you are grieving that happy union that has come to an end sooner than your death or your lifetime.

You are about to discover, that when trauma of any kind hits you, you must go through a healing journey so that you do not bleed on everyone around you. Trauma is defined as a psychological, emotional response to any event or an experience that is deeply distressing or disturbing. The Center for Anxiety also refers to something upsetting, such as being involved in an accident, having an illness or injury, losing a loved one, or going through a divorce. This book will help you to move on with your life without hurting the innocent people around you. This could include your children, family, friends and your future spouse if you decide to find love again. The steps in the book will teach you the stuff that no one has ever been prepared to expect after saying, "**I do**."

Remember that healing is a continuous process. It's very important that I stress this to you. You can skip a meal in real life and survive, but if you skip a stage in the healing process, it will be detrimental in the very near future. This book is a healing manual from the time trauma hits until you find love again.

Some people can serve as distractions or they might be the very same people that hurt you in the first place during the grieving and divorce processes. When you are ready to take healing seriously, you must put on some dark sunglasses, so that you can block some people and some things from your life.

You do not need anyone's approval except your own to go on this healing journey!

Do not be swayed by the "what will people say?" syndrome. It has kept a lot of widows and divorcees living in the painful dark side of life. Holding onto the pain will only make you a prisoner.

This book will prepare you, *to get your groove back,* and if you want to find love again this is the best book for you. It will take you through a step-by-step process on how to prepare yourself for the ever-changing dating world and prepare you to get the love that you still deserve. The healing section is also useful to anyone that has experienced any loss in their life, a relationship breakdown, divorce or even dumped by a guy.

Go on the healing journey, find your purpose and learn to love yourself, so that you can love and be loved again. This will involve you going onto a physical, emotional and psychological detox. What are you waiting for? Be grateful that at least someone loved you enough to take you to the altar and you said **I do** to each other. You will appreciate the process as it will make you a stronger person than you were before. The naysayers will always be there to try and pull you down. This book will give you the wisdom and courage you need to move on with your life. Turning a new chapter in your life does not mean that you do not validate that your spouse is gone, you are celebrating the time you had together with him and now it's time to move ahead with your own life. Remember that he will always hold a special place in your heart no matter what.

This is my gift to you, so you can go through the hurts and pains of widowhood. It has changed the trajectory of your life forever. You will emerge with enough courage to get through the healing process.

YOU GOT THIS AND I GOT YOUR BACK!

Foreword

It was the following morning after my husband died that I found myself sitting on the floor in a corner, surrounded by my family and friends. It finally dawned on me that I was a widow. All I saw was black and I realised then that widowhood has a colour, Black. Now what? My future is now an elusive dream and what about my three children, the youngest was five years old?

The author describes how she was overwhelmed by grief, confusion, anger, frustrations, betrayal, disappointments, and the pain of her loss as she became a widow unwillingly. Time seems to freeze as the widow tries to pick the pieces of what's left. Being a widow is like being an amateur in a brand-new life filled with competent people; a deer in the red lights so to speak. The widow feels numb, lonely, judged and feels like a ton of bricks just fell on her head. It takes lots of strength and courage to wrap her mind around this roller coaster life in front of her.

The author, a widow herself, went through all the stages of grief, encountered setbacks, trials and tribulations and still came out stronger than before. What does not kill you makes you stronger. This is the reason this book was compiled; to show other widows, divorcees, or anyone that has lost anyone in their lives, that healing is possible if you put your mind to it.

She also describes the benefits of healing, versus carrying all that pain in your heart. You can never move ahead in your life without proper healing. We pretend and sometimes lie to ourselves that we have healed, and yet we continue to bleed on everyone around us. This permeates our romantic, social and family relationships. Those wounds from grieving the loss develop into frustrations, resentment, bitterness, hate and paralysing fear.

The author does an excellent job of describing the importance of healing and how to find authentic healing. Once healing is achieved, forgiveness follows. In the widowhood journey, a lot happens. People hurt you and you hurt other people unintentionally. You carry all that junk in your heart and mind and it eats you up day after day. Forgiveness is not saying what happened to you was right. Rather, it helps you to release all that pain and makes the letting go process much easier. Once forgiveness is given and taken, the author shows how the widow's life goes through a transformation and starts to create a new identity for herself.

The author introduces the widow into the new world to find love again. This might seem like a daunting task at first. It's Like asking a fish to climb a tree. The good news is that it is achievable doable. This book provides you with an exceptionally written guide for your new life.

1

ROCK BOTTOM SUCKS

Growing up I never thought that I would experience the most life-changing trauma in my late 30s. Life was great when Temba and I got married officially in 1988. We had a traditional marriage in 1987 and decided to make it official the following year. We met in a grocery store after he knocked my cart over. He admitted afterwards that he just wanted to catch my attention. He had these captivating eyes that melted my heart. Whenever he was fully paying attention, he would tilt his head to one side and he would look into my eyes, nodding his head at the same time. Later in our marriage, I would catch him if he was not paying attention, as he would not give me that head tilt. He was a 6.2" tall and slim guy. He walked with strides like Barack Obama.

Oh my god, he stole my heart! He loved to be dressed up in suits and ties. If he did not have a suit on, he would still wear dress pants (trousers), a shirt and a tie. He never left for work without a tie and never wore jeans to work. Never! Temba was very good with figures and he was a lecturer in the Engineering Department, the head of the Calculation Aided Design (C.A.D.) department. We were married for 12 years, but we were together for thirteen half years.

Soon after our wedding we left the country and went to College in the United Kingdom. We had only had one child, Rue. Upon our return, we brought a red sports car, which was the only one of its kind in the city we lived in. It sure was a head turner and I loved that car. I was known as the lady with the Red sports car. We both taught at the same college and my car had a special parking spot under a tree, as Temba did not want this car to be damaged by any means. He had bought me this car as a birthday present, and to appreciate all the support given to him while he was in school. I graduated earlier than he did, so I worked full time while he finished school.

We got married, for better, for worse and "till death do us part." Little did I know, that things would totally change in a couple of years.

We were together for thirteen and half years and then I got widowed. It felt as if God had failed me. In my mind, I was very angry with God, for letting me down. *"God, how could you let this happen to me?"* I asked repeatedly, and no one was there to give me an answer. The worst part was, I never had a chance to say goodbye to my husband when he died. He was a **victim of circumstances**.

Jealousy amongst Temba's peers played the biggest part in my husband's death. He trusted some people that betrayed him. I will call one of the individuals, "Sandura."

This team of peers became very besotted with our lives. Temba was an aspiring well-spoken and well-educated college lecturer, who had a successful life ahead of him. He and his friend had opened a huge engineering company. Sandura did not want change, so he made a personal vendetta against Temba's life." A lot of resentment, envy, and jealousy were soon stirred up and my husband was caught up in a web of deception and he lost his life.

His death raised a lot of unanswered questions to this day. His family and my family don't really talk about it, because of the circumstances that surround his death. It usually opens many wounds that have healed. Talking about it is like reliving that trauma again. Talking about the way how Temba died, took a lot of courage from me. It's heartbreaking, I will leave it at that, let's move on.

Surprise!

Standing at the altar, marrying the love of your life, no one ever prepares you for when death strikes. Temba left me three beautiful children and the youngest was only five when he passed away. We had plans to build a big five-bedroom house, each child with a bedroom for themselves. It would have our master bedroom, and one bedroom for the visitors and then we would build a small cottage for the childminder and housekeeper.

No one ever prepares you for the role of a widow. It's a role that is dumped on you without your consent. This status is just dumped on your shoulders and you are expected to carry it without any preparation. That's widowhood for you. No one even asks you whether you want to be called by that title or not. People might not address as you, "Hello widow Rose," but be rest assured that it's going to come up in every conversation you have with people. *"Oh, sorry for your loss, oh shame, How so unfortunate,"* are some examples of phrases I heard quite often when Temba passed away.

Being a widow is never an easy lifestyle, as no one is trained for this or the challenges that come with it. When you sign the marriage certificate there is nowhere on it that you sign to be a widow. When you have children, it becomes even harder. You try to be strong, but as the days progress more and more challenges begin to accumulate. These will wear you down bit by bit.

Time freezes at night and sleeping becomes a scarce commodity to a widow. Life becomes dull and it feels like you are in a fog. You feel angry, frustrated and helpless. When my children and I got home from the funeral, my parents came home with us. They gave me all the moral support I needed. When it came night time for some reason time froze. I tossed and turned as all these, **"What If,"** thoughts were running through my mind at gazillion kilometers per hour. **"What if** I cannot cope with this?" **"What if** I cannot take care of our children without my husband?"

When the spouse is gone you have a different title, from wife to a widow. You lose the status you had of belonging to a couple and now you are alone in the world of couples. Just the thought of going through this major life change, caused me to hit rock bottom. It sucks to be in this state as you feel helpless and alone.

Grief Paralysis

When the news that Temba was gone got to me, my brain froze, I got confused, and my body was numb for some time. The clock stopped clicking, and everything else becomes a tough meal to digest. "God this is not what I signed up for," I said to myself. No one had prepared me that death was going to separate us so soon in our lives. Most widows go into this **phase** in which they withdraw and wallow in their grief. You might build a shell around yourself and you feel safe in that zone.

Days after the funeral when everyone else is gone, that's when reality hits home. You become aware that it was not a dream, it actually happened, and you are alone.

Carrying on with life becomes a chore. Normal things like taking a shower can be a daunting experience, as you are not motivated to look good at all. You ask yourself, "What's the point?" Your pillow becomes your best buddy, as it knows how many buckets of tears you shed every day. Your pillow is the only item in your life that can describe your pain as it is drenched with all those tears that involuntarily roll down your cheeks. Crying yourself to sleep, if you can sleep that is, becomes a norm to most widows.

You suddenly have no idea what tomorrow brings for you. You see life through a black veil. Nothing, nobody, can make the pain go away. The pain is beyond giving birth to a child. You need to walk the "***Widowhood Walk***", to understand the depth and the gravity of this pain.

The day when I went to the government building to pick up his death certificate, I thought to myself this is it; he is now addressed as, "the late Temba." Late for what? I kept asking myself. Even to this day I never understand why when a person dies, they are called, "the late." That document is going to be part of you for the longest time as whatever you must do that calls for a Mrs. so, so or Mr. so, so you must produce both the Marriage Certificate and the Death Certificate. I thought to myself now he is a statistic.

Everyone deals with pain or grief differently, some are hit harder than others, but whatever the case might be it does not change that the journey as a widow has started.

Single Parenting

My husband Temba died on July 9th, 2000; it was just after the evening visiting hours. I still remember when that phone call came. The voice on the other side asked to confirm my identity on the phone and I did. There was a long silence and the horrible news was then broken to me. I remember the receiver falling off my hands and I followed it to the floor. That phone call changed my life to this day. I wept like a baby I could not contain myself it was just too much to handle. I did not know what to do and what to think. My family was notified, and my brother arrived a few minutes later. He just gave me a big hug and did not say much to me at that point. I looked at him and said, "How am I going to manage to raise the kids on my own? What is going to happen to me?" He could not answer me. He just looked at me and gave me another hug and said that no one knew what will happen moving forward. He told me to leave everything to God. I was now a widow and a single parent.

Rue, the eldest daughter was supposed to start grade eight the following year at a boarding school. She was 12 years old. Ronnie was nine years old, and the youngest, Ropa, was only five years. Ropa barely remembers her dad to this day. It still breaks my heart to this day when Ropa asks about her dad. Sometimes she asks me how her dad used to laugh, walk, smile and even chew his food. The funny thing is, she walks like her dad, and this still puzzles her. I have seen her a couple of times studying her dad's pictures looking for comfort in the pictures.

When Ropa was in grade nine she came home crying one day. I asked her what was wrong, and she said that they had an exercise in class that day to write about their parents. She said she wrote about mum, but could not write anything about her dad. She said to the teacher that she barely remembered him. So, the teacher thought maybe the father was never in her life. She asked her again what had happened to her dad. She said that's when she started crying and the other kids found it funny, so they laughed at her. We had moved from Zimbabwe to Canada and Ropa was still new at this school. Some kids in her class had found a weapon to bully her with. Sometimes she would ask me the most difficult question like, "Mum how come I am the only one who does not know about my dad in my class?" Even to this day, she still asks a lot of questions about her dad. Ropa never got to understand what happened to her dad.

Sometimes losing a parent when a child is too young to remember anything is worse than, when the child is older, as they can remember what happened to their parent. She spent days refusing to go to school until I had to go to meet her principal about the bullying. Ropa never got a chance to create memories with her dad as the other two did. She has no idea what it feels like to have a dad in her life, to receive a father and daughter relationship. She will never be daddy's little girl. Her life has a big void that I will never be able to fill up. Ropa was the kind of baby that needed her daddy to put her to sleep and would ask for her dad when she wakes up. During the day when she wants something, the first person she would cry and ask for was her dad. So, you can imagine the stress I went through trying to make her understand that daddy is not coming home anymore. The only trick I used for a whole was she loved riding in the car. So, when she would start crying I would take her around the block in the car and she would be snoring in minutes, and I would pray she never wakes up during the night.

Ropa was fortunate enough to be changed from her class. There are a lot of kids like Ropa who are being bullied to the point of taking their own lives. This is one of the challenges that as a widow you will deal with especially if the children are still of school age.

Becoming a widow and a single parent scared me to death. Most widows in my city at that time did not do very well in this phase of their lives. All the parental duties that we used to share like taking to kids to school and picking them up, were now falling on my lap. When one of the children fell ill, it meant I had to go to the emergency alone. It was heartbreaking. I remember when Ronnie graduated high school when we got the Jack Singer Hall, in Calgary. I started to tear up when he was lining up with the other graduates. In my mind, I was thinking, I wish Temba, that you were here to see your son graduate. What joy, it could have brought to him. When Ronnie was walking the stage to get his Diploma I was literally sobbing. I could not control it. It hit me again that I was a single parent and a widow too.

The same painful experience presented itself when Rue had to graduate at the University of Calgary with a B.Sc. Nursing degree. Rue and I were graduating on the same day, and time but different venues and cities. I was torn between missing my graduation and attending her graduation. This is something that both of us worked so hard for. I felt guilty not attending her graduation ceremony and she felt guilty for not attending mine. I remember we both cried as we were both torn. Thanks to my sister, Patience, who showed up unexpectedly to attend Rue's graduation ceremony on my behalf. That was the best surprise ever. When Ropa graduated, it was better because all of us were there to cheer her on. Raising children as a single parent is no joke. You start to think about what will happen when the kids go off course. Who is going to help you put them back on track? Are they going to listen to your parental advice at all? So, many "**what ifs**," go through your mind.

As a single mother, you get overprotective of your children. The children, on the other hand, get overprotective of their mothers. This is the reason that most families that have lost a parent become very tightly knit. Single mothers become heroin to their children. This also puts pressure on you to be perfect and be there for your children all the time. Most of the times I wish people could marry for life, never die, or divorce, and look after their children together.

When a spouse dies, a widow becomes a single parent. I get that. However, you can never be both a mother and a dad at the same time. When Temba was alive, he would make my son's necktie every morning. I had never taken the initiative to learn how to do it. When he passed, I had to learn the hard way. My dad had to move in with me to help me with this tie issue. He had to teach me how to do it. Being a widow and a single parent was a job that I never envisaged in my life. I thought Temba and I would raise our children together and they, in turn, would take care of us in our old age. Sadly no one was going teach my daughters what to expect from men on their first dates, and no one to teach my son how to handle his first date, nor to help him choose his tuxedo on his wedding day. "But why me?" is the question that I asked myself.

Those that are lucky to have their husbands with them have no idea what you and your children are going through. The foundation of your children's life has been shaken with the passing of their dad. These children will never enjoy the love of both parents. It means they are now relying on you for parental love as the surviving parent. This can be hard sometimes, as you can seem to balance this love to everyone as well as yourself.

When the father of your children, your husband dies, be careful what you say to your children, when you are trying to comfort or console them. When Temba passed away, I remember I took my children and we sat in a circle after the funeral. I said to them that I would do my best to take care of them and that they should not worry as I was still there to look out and love them. When my father passed away three years later, Ronnie came to me and said, "Mum don't worry," "GOGO," meaning my mother, is still there and she can take care and love you." You know I looked at him with a blank face and he said, "Mum that's what you told us when our dad passed away, remember?" From that day, I am very conscious of what I say when someone is bereaved as your words will come back to bite you in your face later.

Never make unrealistic promises to your kids, just tell them you will do the best that you can for them. Teach your children not expect too much from you that way when you cannot meet their expectations, they are not devastated. Remember to reassure your kids that you will do your best to be there for them because you are not immortal. Your children still need that strong and solid foundation of parental love and you are all they have left in terms of parental love, support, and guidance. It is very important that your children understand the financial limitations that you will be facing with the passing of their father. If they are old enough to comprehend, they need to understand that you are relying on one income until maybe all the finances have been sorted out with the lawyers or the Government offices. Do the best you can to provide for them and if you cannot afford anything make sure they understand why it is that way. This will prevent children from resenting you as they might think you are not giving them what they deserve. Once they understand your financial situation, they will help you to budget and save money. I did this with my three children. We would walk in the grocery store, Ronnie with the shopping list, and Rue with the calculator, adding up what was in the trolley. This made my life so much easier as they knew how much money we had to spend and how much we needed for living expenses including their school fees.

As a single parent now, you must realize that you no longer belong to the couple's groups you used to be part of. Your married friends will find it odd to invite you to an event that they know they will be attending as couples. I guess they would be trying to protect you from being envious of their relationships. I have no idea. This makes you feel left out. It's like they don't want to socialize with you. Your conversations are going to be very different. Theirs will be filled with what their husbands and kids are doing and yours will be only about you and your kids. You might not be fun to be around, as all you have are sad stories about the struggles you are facing as a widow. Most of the times you feel like a fish trying to climb a tree. You feel like you are a stranger among your friends. I guess since they are not in your shoes, they have no idea what to do or to say to you. Do not hold this against them.

Your Children Have Feelings Too

Learn how to compartmentalize your life with your children. If their dad's passing is not something you can discuss with them due to the gravity of the situation surrounding his death, then wait until they can comprehend the truth. Sometimes sharing too many details with kids when they are still too young to comprehend can traumatize them for life. Ropa my youngest, would always ask for her dad, even after the funeral. I would try to explain to her that dad is not coming back because we left him in the village. She continued to ask why he was in the village and not coming home. It was hard for me to make her understand that her dad was never coming home forever. I would tell her that he went to be with the angels in heaven. I reassured her that he was watching over her and that one day we will all meet again. This made her happy that her dad was watching over her. I guess in her little mind that was enough comfort. At this age, questions will continue to be thrown at you even at some unexpected times of the day and places too. The other two children at least understood what was going on and all they needed was the reassurance that I will continue to love them as before and more since their dad was gone. So, patience is extremely necessary to make sure that the kids understand what happened to their dad.

Soon after the funeral, it might take you some days before you want to go out or back to work. Give yourself and your children that time to just sit at home to process what just happened to your lives. Let the children grieve in their own way. I remember after the funeral the teachers for all my three children were aware that they might miss school for some days. Rue's classmates came home soon after we returned home, from the funeral and we all cried so much, but we were all smiles after they sang for us. We appreciated that gesture of being remembered at the lowest point of our lives. Rues' friends and classmates and their teachers all brought gifts for us. Their message was that we should never forget that there are people that still care and love us, even though our loved one had departed.

Another visit from the school took place some days later. It was a Friday when I got a call from Ronnie's teacher that they were coming to pay their condolences after school. For sure after school, I saw this group of school kids coming through my gate. Minutes later a big knock on the door and 25 of Ronnie's classmates had come to visit us and with wide smiles. They recited the little poems that each one had written for us to comfort us. It was a very touching moment to see these children remember their classmate who had been bereaved. This meant a lot to us. I remember as we all bundled up and made the biggest group hug I had ever seen, with me and the kids in the middle. I felt a lot of love and I could see Ronnie was all smiles that his classmates had remembered him at his moment of need. I think as parents we should teach our children to be there for their friends so that they understand the importance of supporting one another.

One thing we forget as widows is children will need time away from you so that they can recuperate. You also need time away from them as tempers can flare up for no reason as everyone is trying to deal with their loss in a different way. I only realized that I needed time away from my children. My dearest friend, Cecilia, called two weeks after the funeral and said she was coming to pick up the kids. At first, I was very defensive about this and I thought the kids needed me more than anybody else at this time. Yes, it's true, but remember all of us were tired, grieving and nothing new had really happened to us since Temba's passing. Although children are grieving, they all need to have fun besides just grieving. Kids must be allowed to be themselves. So, let them have it. They spent the weekend away from home. When they came back, they were all rejuvenated and were happy to resume life with a new vision. They had life in them and that made me so happy to see that my children had regained their joy to live again. You might say that this sounds crazy Rose. As crazy as it might sound it works and that time apart will make you and them realize how much you love and miss each other. It gives the children another view to life that there are still some people that care for them to take them to their homes. That weekend was very important to us. It solidified my relationship with my children and with my friend, knowing that she loved and cared for me like that. After that, it was like a routine that every month my friend would call or some time just showed up to pick up the children for the weekend. This gave me time to recuperate as well.

2

STUMBLING ALONG

Widowhood never comes with a manual or a-to-do-list. You will learn about this status as you go. I guess when you marry no one expects you to be a widow at all. Have an open mind, as many people will tell you all sorts of things that worked for them. Be watchful of people that give you widowhood or divorcee advice while they are still happily married to their husbands. Take the advice with a grain of salt some of it is helpful though.

12 Things you Need to Know:

1. Does time heal the pain? Time may never really heal all your pain, but you will learn to live with the pain of your loss or marriage. You need time to heal those hurts.
2. The trajectory of your life changes as soon as you become a widow or divorcee. You will never be the same person, never speak the same language (the couple's language). Moving forward, the language is all about you and your children (if there are children involved). Otherwise, it will be back to you and yourself. You will be thrown into a new and strange group of society. A group that you had left upon your marriage. You will have to learn afresh to be single again! You must start to learn how to be on your own and do things without consulting your husband.

3. This new single life sucks. All you wish is that you had never been there at all. It's like you are going backward in life. One day, I remember I was in church and there was this widow who had given her testimony about her life journey. Most people were in tears and after that, the pastor asked all the widows to go forward for him to pray for us. I did not move an inch from my chair. Most people kept looking at me to go to the altar. "I said no," I did not want people to feel sorry for me. I had had enough crying that day I did not want to cry anymore and have people feel sorry for me. It's good, but sometimes it's like you are attention-seeking.

4. You become the black sheep of the family. People will refer to you as, "that widow." It sucks. They even forget that you have a name. Most people soon after the funeral do not really want to be close to you. As if being a widow is contagious. Widows don't have plagues and it's important to fight the stigma. No one ever tells you that people will stare at you like there is something wrong with you. This usually happens when you are in your familiar neighborhood. It's like since you became a widow you became scary. People don't want to be close to you. I am not sure whether it's the widowhood status that just freaks people out or not! Most widows stay out of sight because they try to protect themselves from these crazy stares from people. Some go incognito so people stop staring at them. The worst that can happen is when among those glaring stares they start to whisper behind your back like you have committed some crime of being seen in public when you should be under house arrest or something.

5. When you got married you had tasks to be completed. The difference between the wedding and the funeral is after the wedding the fever about the bride fades away, but the fever around the widow gains momentum after the funeral. People are watching what is going to happen next to this widow and her new life. That fever can go on until you remarry or until you move to a new area where people don't really know you.

6. People will never understand you and what you are going through, so

expect to be misunderstood or taken for granted. Some people will think that they know how to help you when they have zero clues of what is going on in your mind and later alone in your life. People expect you to behave in a certain way. Sometimes people do not get it that your thought process is altered during this time you are grieving. People have no idea that you are also trying to adjust to this new scary, lonely, strange and sad role of a single parent entitled a divorcee or a widow. The only people who can understand you the most, are those that have walked that same road before you as widows, or know someone who has gone through the same predicament.

7. Grief is overwhelming and the pain is beyond description. You can never compare it to anything under the sun. Labor pains come and disappear once the child is born, but the pain of losing someone you love stays with you for the longest time.

8. I faced a lot of betrayal from people that I thought were close to me. I will refer to them as "Those Two." They got hold of the Notice of Death from the hospital where my husband died. They went to the Registry Office and posed like Temba was a single man without a legal wife. The death certificate was provided to them and they went to his insurance company to claim some money from them. Those two people knew about Temba's insurance policies with this company. Unfortunately, the receptionist knew that Temba was legally married to Rosemary and they were asked why they had brought a death certificate that indicated that he was single. They told the receptionist that Temba had been divorced some years back. What they did not know is that when a person is legally divorced, they are given a divorce certificate. That was what saved me. Had I not been legally married they could have taken all the insurance benefits. All this happened when I was still in the village, where my husband had been buried. I was still in mourning and did not even think about getting the death certificate yet. Had Temba not put my name down as a spouse, those benefits would have gone into the wrong hands.

9. So please widows, watch out for things like this. People will try to take

advantage of your vulnerability and take things away from you. I had to go back to the registry office to produce the marriage certificate for this to be corrected. The officer at the registry office had to involve his supervisor to get this mess corrected. The supervisor asked if I wanted to press charges for fraud and I said no, as all I wanted was the death certificate to be corrected so I could start the widow's tasks. I had three mouths to feed and fees to pay for them. I thank God it was all corrected. I had to choose my battles. That battle was not worth fighting and God had even fought that one for me. The fact that the receptionist was able to check the records was a sign of God at work. I learned that life was not going to be a bed of roses for my children and me. I learned to fight and stand for what was mine and what I believed in. I knew that I if didn't stand for myself people were going to walk all over me and take advantage of me. I was labelled the Rebellious Widow!

10. Some people will try to avoid you at all costs. Some people have this impression that you want to ask for favors and cry about your loss all the time. I know sometimes it happens, but not to everyone. I had a situation with tying my son's necktie. It got to a point where I had to ask my dad to come and stay with me because my neighbor's wife was not happy with her husband doing my son's tie every morning. I guess I should have learned how to do it, but because Temba took care of it for me, I never bothered to learn. The funny thing is to this day I have seen some men who cannot make the proper tie knot the right way. I had to make 7 ties and I hang them all made up on hooks in Ronnie's room so that life in the morning was bearable. In the end, my dad had to teach both of us my son and myself how to do the proper tie knot.

11. You lose a sense of time when you are grieving. Nights become extremely long and unbearable.

12. No one tells you that sometimes you become an option in people's lives. Even some of your best friends. Their lives have not been disrupted except yours. You are the only one that is dealing with major changes in life. Sometimes people must take care of their own lives and you must

learn to accept that change too. You feel like you are the fifth wheel to a car. They will only look for you when something goes wrong. This is normal, so accept it and deal with the next issue or challenge. Another devastating thing is, you can lose your support base from some of your family members, your co-workers, the congregation at church, and others. This also happens in your grieving journey.

13. You are never prepared for the stress that comes with losing your spouse. The pain permeates every cell of your body, causing a lot of physiological changes in you. Your cortisol levels rise. You are sleep deprived. Heart rate and blood pressure rise, and it affects your mood too. This will certainly affect your immune system and you become prone to illnesses that you were immune to before your loss. Your body too misses his touch, his feel and your nose will miss his smell, your ears will miss his voice. The list goes on.

I am not here to scare you with all this information, but this is the reality. It might be different for a few people, but for most this is what happens.

Some Insensitive Things People Say

It's not unusual to hear people say some insensitive things. BRACE YOURSELF!

Some might ask you, "So what are you going to do now?" This is infuriating, especially in the early days of your loss. As you have no idea what tomorrow brings for you. Sometimes it takes a lot to explain yourself to people. Smiling usually did it for me. Are you supposed to tell them that you want to run away somewhere, kill yourself or hide?

- How about a person who says to you, "Have a nice day?" How can you respond to that? They know very well you are not having the best of your time. How can I have a nice day? I just buried my husband a couple of days ago and my heart is heavy with grief?
- Oh, he is finally at peace. Really? Do you think I like that he is gone?

What I am supposed to do? It's understood when he has had a long illness, but sometimes people will say the same thing with sudden death.

- "If you need anything let me know I will be here to help." Are you sure about this promise? You can do anything for me? Very vague.

- I'm so sorry to say this to you, you are too young to be a widow. Like I don't know that no one chooses to be a widow. It's dumped on you without your consent, by the way, widows!

- God never gives you what you cannot handle. "Really? Who told you I can handle widowhood?"

- Did he leave you enough money to support the children and yourself? Did he leave you a lot of medical bills? Did you have medical insurance to cover the expenses?

- Are you thinking of remarrying once this is all done?

- What are you going to do with all his clothes, his car, and the business?

- Where are you going to stay? In the same house, are you going to afford it? The house will be too big for you alone.

- You are very strong you are not crying as much as we thought. So, and so was crying like a baby at her husband's funeral, but you are all put together. How are you doing it?

- In all honesty, they meant well, but because of the status of the widow's mind, these statements can seem like insults and rubbing more salt to the wounds. When you don't know what to say to a widow, your precious presence is most welcomed and appreciated. Just being there for the widow with your mouth shut feels more comforting than saying the wrong things that will add injury to a heavy heart.

- Those people that have walked this rocky road will be able to identify with you and know what to say and how to behave. I have been there, and I know how I felt. People will react differently to grief. So, what I went through might be totally different from what you are going through. So, take what you can and use it on your new journey.

- The best thing anyone can say would be, "I have no idea what you are going through right now. Let me know how I can help." This will mean another world to the widow. It shows that people are conscious of the gravity of your pain and are respecting your space and pain.

The Widow's Tasks

The widow's tasks are the things that you will have to take care of in order to settle your husband's estate and take care of everything that pertains to his passing.

Documents to Carry Around with You

- Death Certificate.
- Marriage Certificate, if not anything to show that you were living together if it's a common-law marriage.
- A Will, if it's available. If it's not available, then go to the courthouse and apply for a Grant of Administration in order to be able to access the funds. This can take time depending on the amount of money involved. I had to go to the High Court of Zimbabwe to get the Certificate of Administration. This took almost four months to be released. This is the document that is taken to the pensions office and the pension office also took more than six months for the benefits to be finally released.
- Your IDs, his IDs and kids' IDs (this includes his driver's license, passport, His health card, social security card, national identity card).
- Insurance policies.
- Employment Details.
- Car registrations and their insurances.
- Property titles for houses, condos, etc.
- Bank details, credit cards, line of credit and debit cards.
- Information on good lawyers who can deal with all the paperwork for you, if you are financially stable.
- Any bills to be paid.
- His belongings, like his clothes etc.

Things You Need to Do

1. Take care of the financial details first as you need to know how you will take care of yourself and the children. If you cannot do this, hire a lawyer for a fee. Most of the times it's straightforward.
2. Settle your housing situation. Where are you going to be living now that you are a single mother if there are children involved? If there are no children, you still need to figure out where you will live. Are you going to stay in the same house, or neighborhood or move to a cheaper and smaller place?

Some women feel the need to change houses to get a new start, as the old place could bring painful memories. I stayed in the same house, as it was easier for me to remain in the same house. The house was closer to all the facilities and closer to my job as well. Do what works for you as everyone is different.

1. Have copies of documents. Every place you go to settle the estate, they will ask for his Death Certificate, Marriage Certificate, your IDs, his ID, and children IDs if any.
2. Pay off any debts including the hospital bills.
3. Take care of his belongings. In my culture, the husband's family usually decides what they will do with his belongings. It's not up the widow to decide.
4. Make assessments of any assets you had, like land, houses, businesses and cars.
5. Decide what to do with the rings. Some widows wear their rings around their necks, some keep them on if they have no intention of remarrying again.
6. Deal with any tasks that may crop up as you go.

The "Firsts" of Everything

How do you deal with the first times you have to deal with situations that you used to deal with together with your spouse?

I have categorized them in two sections:

1. **The Unplanned Firsts**
2. **The Calendar Firsts**

The Unplanned Firsts

There are those first experiences that you never plan. They are the surprises, good, bad and sometimes funny.

- The first time you come home after the funeral. Where do you start? What do you do with yourself? It's normal not to do anything those few days when you get back home. You are still going through the trauma of losing your husband and you need time to rest and recollect your scattered mind.
- The first day back to work for me was strange. Everyone was just looking at me, it felt weird and very uncomfortable. I went into my office and I locked myself in there for hours. I felt like I did not belong there anymore. We both used to lecture at the same college, so it was hard going back without him.
- First time I had a flat tire on the highway coming from my parent's home. I had no idea how to change a tire, let alone know where the spare tire was. Looking at the wheel spanner was like looking at a horror movie. You know, I laughed at myself thinking, "Where am I going to start." It was getting dark and I had my three children in the car. I tried to wave down cars for help no one stopped to help. Then it dawned on my son that he had seen his dad remove the spare wheel from the trunk of the car. He is the one that showed me where to check for the tire and we struggled to lift the car with the jack. Hours later we managed to change the tire and we were on our way. You know it's always nice to learn

some things and not always rely on your husband to do things for you, because when he is gone you are in big trouble.

- If you used to go to church together. That first service is going to be extra-long for you, as you just want to leave and lock yourself in your house.
- First time on a date. For the young widow, you might choose to find love again. This is very normal. We were made to love and to be loved, but you must be fully ready to date again. When you still feel guilty about dating and feel as if you're cheating on your late husband, then you still need time to heal your heart. If you feel excited to move on, then why not start dating. It will feel awkward at first and the thing is you might start comparing your late husband to the new Mr. in front of you. This can be very unfair to the new Mr Finding Love, who might have never dated a widow before. So, go easy on him. More about dating in Chapter 12.

The Calendar Firsts

Then there are those that come along on the calendar days, like birthdays, wedding anniversaries and so on. The order will depend on when your spouse passed away.

- For me, it was our wedding anniversary. He passed away in July and our wedding anniversary was in August. This was a painful reminder of my new status as a widow. Now I had to choose which date to remember the most, our wedding anniversary, or Temba's date of death, or both?
- Soon after Temba's funeral came the first college graduation ceremony. He used to be a college MC. So, imagine my feeling when someone else was emceeing the ceremony. I was in tears at the beginning of the ceremony when they had a moment of silence for his passing. Really, he was supposed to be giving the speech, but he is no more, and they were talking about him in the past tense. It was tough.
- Then September came my first birthday, without him. He used to take me out and spoil me with surprises. Now, who was going to do this for

me? On my birthday, my children made breakfast in bed for me. Later we went out for a drink. It was nice of them to have saved the little pocket money they had and made my day special. The kids were also good at arranging some surprises for me. When we got to the hotel, my best friend was there, waiting for me with a big bunch of roses.

- The first school holidays came in September. We used to drive to the village. We would go to his village first, where his parents lived, and spend a few days. Then we would drive to my parent's homestead, where I grew up. So now, where was I supposed to go first? To go to his village was going to open wounds because I would have to visit his grave, which I did not mind at all. You know it was one of those decisions that I had to make as well. So, we started to go to his village and put flowers on his grave and then we went to my village last. The thought of driving myself the whole journey was tough, as Temba would have done most of the driving. If you were in my shoes where would have gone first?

- Then the first Christmas holiday without Temba. I had no money to buy my children big gifts. I had explained to them not to expect much from me that Christmas. What I could afford for them was a million dollars for them. This is the advantage of making sure that the children understand your financial dilemma after the death of their dad. There was just a big delay in his estate settlement. That took a big toll on my finances.

- The following year was the first term for the year, the opening of the College. We used to have a big assembly welcoming all the new staff members and the new students, and Temba again would have been the MC. That was another blow to my heart right there.

- Then came Ropa's first birthday, Rue's birthday and lastly Ronnie's birthday. My children's birthdays came the following year as they are all born before July, the month in which their dad passed on. The first birthdays were hard for everyone and you can imagine how the children felt. There are not enough words you can say to console a child when he or she wishes their dad was there on their special day.

- Your first Valentine's day will come and go and somehow you just wish if he was there to send that bunch of red roses again.

The Widow's Dress Code (In Zimbabwe)

Tommy Canvas Tennis Shoes

The widow outfits differ from country to country, and culture to culture. In Zimbabwe, widows are supposed to wear all black from head to toe. The widow's head was supposed to be covered with a head tie or "Dhuku," scarf or turban. Most of the times the in-laws would buy the black cotton material and get a tailor to make a pleated dress with a collar. From that material then a headscarf would be made as well. Sometimes the dress would have side pockets. It was also meant to be a long dress, to go midway between the knees and the ankles. To top it off, they would buy black canvas tennis shoes called, "Tommy," from Bata Shoe Company (as seen in the picture).

This gave the widows that miserable, poor, unhappy, grieve stricken and attention-seeking look. It also drew the attention of many people as heads would turn, when a widow passed by. If a widow was a working woman, then the in-laws would be lenient and ask her to wear black outfits, still, head to toe. What still baffles me is that, it's only widowed women who must be stuck with the black grief-stricken outfits for a whole year. For men, you never know that they are widowed until they mentioned it.

My dad refused to have me wear this pity-seeking outfit. I was lucky I did not have to wear it. He told my in-laws that Rosemary is a college lecturer, and the outfit would make me look like a fish out of water. I remember my in-laws saying that it was the culture of the family. My dad still said no to it and he stuck to his guns.

This widow outfit made most widows look older and pathetic. The outfit was a reminder of your painful loss for the whole year that you were supposed to wear it. It was an identity outfit. If you were lucky then two dresses would be made for you. If not, it was that one dress that you wore day in and day out until one year after the death of your husband. The in-laws have a ceremony at their homestead. They would ask you to hand over that black widow's outfit and they would burn it. If the in-laws take their time to organize this ceremony, then the widow had no power to remove it. This was one of the cultural rules that I still struggle with. Why does this only happen to women? I asked my dad and he said its only very conservative families that still do this. Nowadays with women emancipation advocacy, things have changed a little. Widows still face a lot of hardship and discrimination from their in-laws and society in general.

3

THE AFRICAN/INDIAN
WIDOWHOOD

In Igboland, Nigeria, the widow's mourning of the dead husband is viewed as a very important tradition which the living spouse must observe in honour of the dead. When the husband of the woman dies, the mourning begins at that moment of his final breath. The bereaved wife runs about wailing at the top of her voice. A prominent feature is the intensity of wailing, weeping, and hysteria which death generates or is expected to generate. The children would join in the wailing together with other friends and relatives of the family. In their wailing, they would regret a big loss as they recount the deceased's life achievements, his love, and faithfulness as a good, honest, reliable brother, husband, father or uncle. After this stage, the wife becomes the focus in terms of mourning the departed husband.

The widow must be made to tie a cloth on the body of the late husband. In some parts of Igboland like Onitsha, the divorced wife of the man must return to mourn the man and do posthumous reconciliation with the man in the presence of the matrilineal daughters (umuada), otherwise, she is believed to be in danger of the ghost of the deceased man. The wife (or wives, if he was a polygamist) of a titled man is (are) not allowed to cry or make any noise until the proper arrangement is made. This means that the widow must suppress the natural psychological grief in her for some days simply because her husband was a titled person.

In general, the Nigerian or Zimbabwean widow would be sat on a big mattress, surrounded by pillows and cushions, or she would be sat on a plain mat without any pillows, but with some blankets. The *Female elders* surround the widow, commanding her to make sure she obeys the rules of mourning rites. The in-laws and their family and friends will be watching to see the depth of the Widow's mourning. Is she crying loud enough, and is it pathetic and loud enough to keep the weight of her loss almost tangible?

In some parts of Nigeria, from that moment the husband died, the widow is believed to be unclean, and likely to contaminate herself and others. Therefore, no one touches her except her fellow widows, who are equally believed to be defiled. She is given a piece of stick to scratch herself in case of natural body irritation, and oil palm chaff (avuvu *nkwu*) to wash her hand periodically in order to reduce her uncleanness. She is also not allowed to eat any food bought for the funeral ceremony. It is feared that she will die if she eats such foods. Hence, her food during the funeral ceremonies is cooked separately.

The days before the burial of the husband are always horrible for the widow, this was true in Zimbabwe too. She is made to stay awake in the same room with the corpse. If he died in the village without any mortuary services, she is required to be waving away flies from perching on the fast decomposing corpse. Every morning she is supposed to raise an early morning cry before anybody is awake and this continues until the day of the burial. The relatives made sure she stays awake all night with her bitter kola (aku *ilu*) in her mouth. This is to remind her of the bitterness of the death of her husband. Furthermore, if the widow had a disagreement with the husband shortly before his death, the widow will be made to lie with the corpse for many hours and in addition pay heavily in cash as a fine. This is torture for sure. How much pain does a widow have to endure? After the burial, the widow now puts on the real black cloth for the rest of the mourning period which is supposed to last for a year as a sign of grief and love for the departed husband. In the Zimbabwean culture, the widow will put the black widow's outfit.

In this year, the widow is not allowed to date or have sex with anyone. This is taboo, as it is believed that you are still unclean and still married to the late husband. After the one year, the day after the cleansing ceremony, she exercises her restricted liberty as she is received back into the family and can now cook what others can eat and have the freedom to talk to people.

In Zimbabwe and Igbo culture, the mourning experience is dehumanizing, discriminatory against women, antisocial, unlawful and oppressive. In some African countries, widows get their heads shaved as a sign of mourning and respect for the dead husband.

In India, widows are placed in shelters far away from their matrimonial homes.

Photo Credit: Rebecca Conway for the New York Times.

This widow is around 75, but cannot return to her home due to the abuse she fled years ago. She still thinks about returning to her family. *Photo Credit: Rebecca Conway for The New York Times.*

Other shelters for widows, in India, run by non-profit organizations, are less inviting, with stained walls and bare, concrete rooms, but some widows say they prefer staying in them because they provide higher pensions. They get a roof over their heads and are not subjected to abuse from their families and the in-laws.

At government-run ashrams, women are given just a few hundred rupees each month, or less than $10 — and payments are sometimes delayed by weeks. Most widows in the remote parts of India are poor and illiterate. When the spouse dies, they're regarded as a burden to the families and are treated as castaways who have lost their social values in society.

Photo Credit: Rebecca Conway for the New York Times

This Widow (in the picture above), lives in one of the widow's camps where they are kept poor and dressed in white saris. The white saris are a signifier that color has been drained from their lives as a sign of bereavement. It shows that they have nothing left for them and are worthless. One wonders why the world still treats other human beings so cruelly, simply because the husband is dead.

Husband's Pension Benefits

After about nine months or more after the funeral, my husband's pension benefits were finally released. When the pension benefits were deposited into my account, I did the noble thing of withdrawing about $13.000 and bought some groceries for my in-laws. I visited my in-laws in the village. When I got there, I felt this heavy emptiness in me. The memories of the funeral were still vivid in my mind. I looked over and saw my husband's grave, still as a heap of soil and the flowers I had brought a couple of months before were still there. I started weeping quietly. My kids noticed that I was weeping. They all gathered around and gave me this huge group hug and told me to be strong for them.

The parents' in-laws were home when my children and I got there. We took out the groceries I had brought for them. I helped my mother-in-law to make the fire and helped prepare the food, so we could have lunch together. When all was done, we cleaned up the kitchen and everyone was in a happy mood at that moment.

It was at this time an opportunity presented itself for me to tell them about the pension benefits, and we all sat down on the kitchen floor. My father-in-law had sent a message to his brother who lived just a few houses from theirs about our visit. He was also there in the kitchen. So, I took out the envelope with the $13.000 and I gave it to my son to hand over to my mother-in-law. I told them that their son's pension benefits had been released, and I had taken some of it and brought it for them. My father-in-law said that he was happy with the gesture and said that he felt honored that I had thought of sharing it with them. My mother-in-law was not too happy about that, apparently. She did not even acknowledge the gesture I made to bring the money. She turned to me and said in a stern voice, "Where is the rest of the money? How much did you get? You were not supposed to keep that money. You were supposed to bring it to us, and we were going to give you monthly, however much you needed to pay for school fees and food for the kids. Did you even tell your brother-in-law about this? You should have come here with him. He was the one that was supposed to give us the money, not you!"

Wow! I looked at her in utter amazement! Here I was, thinking that I had done well to bring the money and even tell them that the pension benefits were out. I was very disappointed. I told her that I did not think it was a must for me to let them know how much I had gotten. I still had three young kids to look after and that money was not even enough to send the kids to college, let alone feed them until they were 18 years old.

Tears just started streaming down my face. My father-in-law and his brother intervened. They both said that it was okay for me to keep the money and look after the children. This is when I realized that life will never be the same without my husband. I was devastated. I left the village much-wounded, with a heavy heart, disappointed and carrying a very deep sense of sadness. I asked myself, "Who does that?" Instead of going back to my house I decided to go over to my parents' house.

We arrived just before midnight and my mother knew something was not right. When I got out of the car, I burst into tears and my mother came running asking what had happened. I just needed to feel loved, comforted, to be told it was going to be ok and that I had done an honorable thing. Everyone needs that mama hug, no matter how old you are. When I explained what had transpired at my in-law's homestead, my dad was furious. He said that he did not expect that reaction from my mother-in-law. My mother-in-law had mentioned before that she was not happy with the fact that my dad had refused for me to wear the Black Widow outfit. Serious, I had no idea why she had reacted the way she did. After a while, I realized that she thought I was the rebel daughter-in-law, as I had refused to bring the money to her. So, I felt that she thought I was not honoring the death of her son enough by not wearing the Black Widow outfit.

The things that widows must endure during their widowhood journey are painful. So, what is your story?

What did you learn from my experience shared so far? Is your story worse than mine or vice versa?

I have learned that bad experiences will make some widows bitter and cause them to be resentful towards their in-laws. It is because of these experiences that widows end up bonding with their baggage.

4

DON'T BOND WITH YOUR WIDOWHOOD BAGGAGE

Bonding with your **Widowhood** baggage is when you let your grief run away with your happiness. You let the widowhood status consume most of who you are. Instead of being known by your first name you become the Widow, Queen of Pity Parties. You get to be known for your unhappy life and you become part of the unhappy identity. You get stuck in your sorrow and you are unable to see an end to this pain of **Widowhood.**

Three months after Temba had passed away, we had a memorial service for him. This was held at the village where he was buried. I spoke to my brother-in-law to let him know that I wanted to have the Salvation Army Brass Band from my church to play for the service. He agreed with it since they did not have a chance to be present at the funeral. He even asked how many people he would expect to come from my church. So, I told him that there were about 25 members including the youth choir and the Corps officer (the Pastor), to help with the singing for the band. I sent him the receipts of all the bookings for the 30-seater bus that was going to ferry this band to the village.

The night before we traveled for the memorial service, everything suddenly changed, when I called to finalize everything. My brother in law was a little aloof with me and very abrupt. He told me that I had to cancel the plans to bring the band from my church and my Corps officer. I asked why and he just said that no one had allowed me to bring that band for the memorial service. I was stunned and I thought maybe I misunderstood. I tried to call him back and he was no longer picking up my phone. I thought maybe he was just stressed out with everything that was going on with the loss of his younger brother. I was not sure what to do. I tried to speak to my younger brother-in-law, and he said that he had no idea what I was talking about. So, I was confused as to what was going on and what to expect when we get to the village.

We got to the village a little after 8.00 pm on this fateful Friday night in October 2000. We had to wait for some band members to get off work. Arriving at the homestead, the band members got out of the bus, and they were singing and playing their instruments just happy that they had arrived safely. I was shocked when I was told that the band members and myself, were not welcome there. I felt my stomach turn and asked my brother in law why things had changed from what we had agreed upon. He said he been instructed by their parents. I found out that one of the younger brothers-in-law had fabricated a story that the minibus carrying the band members belonged to my boyfriend. I had seen this brother-in-law check the name on the bus. This minibus belonged to Makunike Omnibus Company, and it was from Mbizo 19 in Kwekwe. I did not know the owner of this omnibus personally. I was referred to his company through a friend (Cecilia) who had used his services before. Now I was being accused of being disrespectful and dishonoring my in-laws and my late husband. I was in shock, like where did all this come from? Why would I do such a thing? My parents were there with me and they tried to explain to the in-laws that it was all lies. I confronted the brother-in-law concerned and asked him why he had done this. He could not answer me. I only found out later, that it was all a set up to embarrass and humiliate me for reasons known to them. This boiled down to the issue that my father had refused that I wear that black widow's outfit. According to them, I had been a radical daughter-in-law, and this was done to embarrass my whole family. I was devastated by this whole fiasco.

Why would people be so mean to another human being and a woman that had given them three beautiful grandchildren?

Why would people be so conniving and mean? The following morning came, and nothing had changed. When I tried to talk to my mother-in-law, she was adamant that she had nothing to do with the decision to turn us away. In the end, my dad just asked me and the band to leave. My dad told my in-laws that what they had done was so uncalled for. They were ill-treating me because I was not following tradition by not wearing the black widow's outfit.

I remember my dad holding my hand and leading me to the minibus saying to me, "Rose your husband is gone, so don't expect any of these people to love you and protect your image." After that, the minibus and all my other relatives that had come from the different parts of the country left. My mother had also brought her church members from my village including their Corps officer (Pastor).

In some cultures, widows are treated like a piece of trash if they don't follow tradition. I had heard stories of widows that had property, children, and money taken away from them. It never crossed my mind that I would be in this compromising situation too. These were, some of the mind-blowing and heart-wrenching events in my **Widowhood** journey. This added to the reason that kept me holding onto my **Widowhood** baggage. I just felt that I was a victim of circumstances and could not get over why my brother-in-law had turned against me like that. I had helped to raise these guys by sending them to school and buying clothes for them. Two of the younger brothers-in-law had moved in with us, soon after our marriage. To this day, it's still a mystery why this brother-in-law fabricated that story.

Misery and sadness became my life. I was stuck in that zone for a while. I felt as if God had let me down. At this stage of my widowhood journey, months had passed by and still no sign of healing and moving ahead for myself. It was hard to move on because two years down the line my father passed away. My dad was my pillar. He was there for me throughout my husband's ordeal. Life without him was just unthinkable, I felt safe with him around. After that, I had to move to North America in the same year, 2003.

My children had to remain behind since I could not secure visas for them at that time. This was the hardest decision I had ever made in my life. A decision to move had to be made, so I could start a new life for my children. In the process of all this, I was separated from my children for almost **six years** before we got reunited. This was hard for all of us, but it had to be done. I would cry at night and had sleepless nights thinking of what could happen to my children. It was a long wait before they joined me.

Before I could even heal, another brother died in 2008, followed by two of my best friends whom I had grown up with. I felt like the world had abandoned me. I was alone, once more. I could not wrap my head around all these losses that kept on piling up on me. I slid into another period of grief and soon again I hit rock bottom. I was drowning in pain and I could not help myself anymore. Instead of looking for help, I thought the pain would suddenly go away. I was too broken to even look around for help and get myself out of all this misery.

Queen of pity parties

"Most people never heal, because they stay in their heads, replaying corrupted scenarios."
S. Mcnutt.

Being sad and isolated became the norm at one point in my life, just after I moved to North America. I would go to my three jobs and come home to sleep. My focus was on making enough money to bring my children over. Taking care of me became a luxury as I could not have time to do it. Neither could I heal properly from all the loss that had befallen me. Sometimes I would break down at work for no reason. I had so much pain that talking about it became too much for me. It felt better just labelling myself as a person who had been plagued by death. Why did I keep losing all these people that mattered so much to me? Why me? Why me?! I could not find any answer. Wallowing in my pain became my relief. It felt better not to talk about it. I felt sorry for myself as no one would understand what I was going through. So, it was easier to just stay away from people and focus on my three jobs and saving money for my kids to come and join me.

Worrying about my children was my daily norm. What would become of them, was my daily fear? I was many thousands of kilometers away from them. I had sent all of them to boarding schools and it was easier that way. It came to a point where I would talk to myself, trying to answer all these questions in my mind. What if anything happened to me while I am so far away? My children would be orphans! What if something really did happen to me, then what? What was going to happen to them? The separation was gruesome.

I made the situation worse by watching all these sad movies in which some orphaned children would have their lives drastically changed after their parents passed away. The guardians who were taking care of those orphaned children had abused their benefits, leaving these children destitute. "What if my children would fall into the same category?" I would ask myself all these unanswered questions. I tried to talk to one lady at work one day. I told her about my coming to North America and leaving my children behind. She went off on the worst guilt trip ever. She told me she would never leave her kids behind and she would decide to stay with the kids no matter what. In my mind, I was thinking, "Did I make the wrong decision to leave my children behind?" I really wanted to stay with my children, but the situation called for me to leave.

It felt like it would never end. I kept asking myself why I could not get a break. I did not seem to see any hope in my situation. If you are an immigrant, you will understand what I mean. It's tough enough getting through the immigration process. Life was dark for me. Wallowing in my pain became better than trying to explain my life to people who will in turn judge that I was not a good mother. I was not a very happy person during this time. I felt there was no use of even going out with workmates for anything. Having fun was like climbing Mount Kilimanjaro, torturous! This usually happens when you let grief overtake your life.

The "what if" Zone

The, "What if" phrase, became my language in my daily thoughts. My mind was clouded with all these terrible things that could happen to me anytime.

I would think, what if I get a call that my children had been killed in some accident?

What if I was killed here in North America? Who will pay for my body to be repatriated to Zimbabwe?

What if I made the wrong decision to leave my children behind?

What if I could not bring my children over and I could not return home to see them?

What if I manage to raise the money and they decide that they did not want to come here?

What if on their way to North America they get lost in one of the airports since they have never flown alone before?

What if they got abducted on their way here?

What if they come here and I find out that, I don't know who they are anymore and vice versa?

My life was a heap of endless misery.

The grief felt endless. "Why could I not find healing? What was wrong with me?" It felt like I had failed myself. All these outrageous self-limiting thoughts started creeping in, that I might never be happy again. The times I went to the mall and saw families together was a trigger for me. I would start crying. I missed my children so much and the pain was so insurmountable. This deep aching pain grew by the day. I missed my husband, my father, my brothers, and everyone else that had passed away as well as, my other siblings. I missed that family unity. My pain became familiar to me and I had given up on finding help for myself. I started thinking that I was meant to be this way until maybe my children came, then I would find comfort in them.

The process of being rejoined with my children took six years and it required a lot of money to pay for the paperwork. All in all, I paid about $7000.00 and the flights for the three children $4350.00. This immigration process added more fuel to my already wounded heart and my recovery journey was not easy. I had no time to relax or to have fun as I had to focus on saving those thousands of dollars to bring my children over. The dream that I had before coming to North America about the good and happy life, soon became elusive. I had to work even harder than I did when I was back home.

At work, I would sit in the cafeteria with people laughing around me and would not find any humor in whatever was going on. I would be in a world of my own. The dark world of grief had overtaken my life to a point where at one point I thought living was pointless since I could not see myself being rejoined with my children. I had held onto the pain so much, that the weight had eradicated my self-worth; my self-esteem had plunged to zero. When you allow grief to overtake your life, you lose joy in living. Anger and frustration started to build and the next thing, I was walking like a time bomb waiting to explode. I thought that I would wake up one day and the pain would have magically disappeared. Sometimes, I felt that this endless pain belonged to me, as I was a widow and widows are supposed to be: -

- Overwhelmingly sad,
- Confused
- Have no ambition to improve their lives
- Angry
- Lose their purpose in life
- Feel worthless
- Feel frustrated
- Sleep-deprived
- Fearful
- Have no appetite (how could I eat when I had no idea whether my children had eaten a meal or not)
- Powerless
- Hopeless

- No confidence
- Feel for sorry myself
- Have no sense of humor

Do any of these, ring a bell to you? You could be like me that got stuck in this wallowing zone.

My solution at the time was that I thought I had to be friends with people that had lost either their husbands, their parents and had none of their children with them. I felt I would belong to that group of people. Thinking back now this was absurd. During that period, it made sense to me.

There are times when your mind runs away with you. You will find yourself creating all these barriers for yourself. You might find it hard to allow other people who might be able to help you. Since they do not fit your narrow-minded, self-limiting beliefs you will be stuck in your own sorrow. This narrow mindedness had made me throw away the most important thing of all, my happiness, my joy, my sanity, and my peace. I was not being kind to myself, neither was I being a good mother to my children. To make matters worse, my children had no idea I was going through all this. Telling them was only going to make their situation worse. The only person who knew was my mother. Every time I spoke to her, I would break down and cry.

Now I believe that when you grieve, be mindful of how and for how long you have been wallowing in your grief. Ask yourself, what good has it brought to your life? If crying is not changing your situation, then you need to refocus and think again. I had held onto my own **Widowhood** baggage for so long, it started to feel normal to me.

5 Myths About Healing

Myth 1: You Are Defined by the Depth of Your Wounds/Pain

Being a widow during early 2000, was too much to handle. I believe someone out there who is reading this now is the same boat I was in. Healing from all this pain seemed impossible. I had become numb to it. Most widows

I had known were still wallowing in their grief years after their husbands had passed away. I thought it was permanent for me too. The **Widowhood** status had permeated in my veins and the cells of my body to a point where it was encompassed in my mind as well. It became part of me.

This hindered my dating life, as I still had some crazy idea that the history of widowhood would repeat itself. Is there anybody out there who believes this is true or who can identify with this? This state of mind is self-destructive. The sad thing is when you are stuck in this mindset, it becomes true and normal for you. I had no idea that holding onto my **Widowhood** baggage was a self-inflicted psychological pain which as a result got stuck in my subconscious. It was like I was falling into a bottomless pit headfirst.

Repressing the pain felt comfortable. I had no idea how to relate to people without pouring my heart out. I kept shifting the pain to other people. I had been hurt and betrayed so bad with so many people, and I could not heal from the grief. Putting it away was safer for me, as I did not have to deal with it. The only problem came when it was triggered by life events, like seeing the family having a good time together.

Myth 2: Once you are Healed You become Independent and no Longer Act and Live Like a Widow

I am sure you are like so what's wrong with that? In my case, I felt moving on meant I was not taking the death of my husband seriously. I was not supposed to be rid of this **Widowhood** pain. Is this crazy at all? Do you identify with this? The mistake I made was that I never talked to anyone about healing from this pain. You know there is a saying which says, *"Birds of the same feather flock together."* I was hanging around all these people that did nothing else but cry about their losses. Being part of this group, made me belong to something and somewhere. Taking the initiative to change was not in me at all and it never crossed my clouded mind at all.

Myth 3: Pain Caused by Widowhood Although Destructive, is Legitimate

Mourning my husband anyway I felt like it made it feel comfortable. It meant that I could hang onto this pain for as long as I saw it fit and comfortable. I felt it was okay to walk with my head buried in the sand so no one could see who I was. If there was no quick fix to this pain, then why bother even going through the healing process? What if I lost someone again in the healing process? So, what's the use?

My quick fix was crying myself to sleep and going through all the bad events that kept following me. Every time I cried, I felt better afterward, without any other solution at hand to solve my issues permanently. Most widows fall into the habit of taking sleeping medications, so that they can get some sleep, to get comfort from that good night's sleep. In the end, some get hooked to these medications and because of no other coping skills fall into the dark hole of addictions. Fortunately, I did not get onto this route.

Myth 4: Loss Causes Ill Health, Both Physically and Emotionally.

When you lose someone you love, you go through a lot of emotions. I went through a lot of physical physiological health issues like fatigue, muscle aches, high blood pressure, etc. The negativity that your body is exposed to, causes all these illnesses.

So according to me, it was normal since most widows and those that suffered a serious divorce were still going through this roller coaster of feeling and hurts. In the meantime, at the back of my mind, I still thought something was not right but could never put a finger on it.

Myth 5: There Is No True Healing or Change from the **Widowhood** Pain

When you feel lost in your pain it never crosses your mind that one day you will be free of all the pain from grieving. You might feel as if healing is too farfetched or off limits for you and you might never think about it. Healing can feel like it's too much work to even think about it, as that would require some major changes in your normal life. I hope anyone never gets to this point as this can be a base for a serious nervous breakdown. I guess this is called the denial stage in grieving. The more you ask yourself the "Why Me", the deeper you sink into your denial state. I just could not accept that at my age in my 30 thirties I was a widow already.

What Is the Truth About Grief/ Loss?

Grief or loss is when you lose someone or something you love. Grieving is a natural process of dealing with your pain for your loss. This could be any one of the following:

- Death of a loved one
- Job loss
- Divorce or relationship breakup
- Retirement/laid off
- Loss of an investment
- Serious terminal illness
- Loss of property

The pain can be overwhelming and sometimes you cannot deal with it. It seems endless and beyond explanation. As I mentioned before dealing with grief has a lot of negative impact on you. So, my advice is when you feel you cannot handle the pain, seek professional help before it's too late. There are healthy ways to deal with your grieving process and talk to someone to help you to find new meaning to life. Everyone reacts differently to pain. Two people could lose a husband at the same time, but the underlying factors that caused the death of the spouse could be the main reason causing the grief. Sometimes the relationship between the spouses can also add to the gravity of the grief.

Misguided Myths about Grieving

Myth 1: Mourning should only take less than a year

We should bear in mind that there was never a limit placed on a grieving process as every individual is different. The only thing you should be mindful of that grieving is not meant to be permanent. Look around you and see how much your grieving has affected people you love or yourself. Ask your unbiased sources to give you an honest opinion.

Myth 2: Not crying out and wallowing in your pain means that you are not really grieving

This is true in the real world. Most of these situations are forced on widows by culture or society. Otherwise, people must be free to grieve in a way that is comfortable for them. Some people can grieve emotionally and be torn up inside and never shed a tear on the outside.

Myth 3 Sometimes you must show that you can hold it together while grieving.

Well, good for you if you can hold it together. Other people cry publicly while others just sob uncontrollably. There are no set rules on how people should grieve. I guess we should be mindful of different cultures that have different ways of grieving and mourning their loved ones.

Myth 4 Starting a new life after your loss means you are ignoring and forgetting the spouse you lost

This is so untrue. If you decided to move on, then it means you have accepted your loss and acknowledged it. You have decided to start a new life with someone else. Life still goes on. This is common in some cultures where, the widows are bound to this myth, but the men can marry anytime when they are ready. This is so unfair to the women though. Most of the time it's the in-laws that force this on the Widows as they feel like you are forgetting about their late loved one.

5

WAYS TO COPE WITH GRIEF

1. Acknowledge the pain or loss.
2. Acceptance of the pain or loss. Be aware that grief might be triggered by a lot of things e.g. songs, certain smells, sounds, and places too. It's best to face these and be able to accept them and move on so that they do not trigger you soon.
3. You are unique and you will deal with it differently. Stop comparing yourself to others. You came into this world alone that's why there is only one of you.
4. Grieving is very different from being depressed. So, when you feel you want to give up on life or life is overly overwhelming, please seek professional help before the death of your spouse claims another person, YOU.
5. Never ignore changes in your emotions, physical health, and psychological health, as these go hand in hand.

The 5 stages of grieving

1. Denial – "This cannot be true", "Not to me," or "Is this a dream?" statements. You refuse to accept it's true.
2. Anger - "Why did this have to happen to me?" "But why can anyone

not answer me?" You are angry about why it happened to you and not someone else.

3. Bargaining - "If it goes away, I will be........." Nice to my husband or Spouse. Or, "I will be a better spouse ......"

4. Depression- "This is so overwhelming," "The burden is too much to carry,"

5. Acceptance- "This is true, but it will change with time and I will be okay. No matter what."

How Do you Know That you are Grieving?

What do you feel?

- Disbelief and Shock.
- When grieving you can go through a lot of emotions. Your brain can race faster than your heart or it can stand still and not allow you to think at all. You can be numb; this is when you do not accept nor deny the loss. You ask a lot of questions as to why it happened.
    - Sadness
    - There is an overwhelming sadness in your heart. You feel like your heart has been ripped into pieces. You find no humor in life.
    - Guilt
    - You may look back and wish you could have done something differently to show how much you loved them. Maybe there is a medical procedure that you felt was too much for the loved one to go through and suggested against it. When they die, that thought will remain on your conscience.

Be mindful when you grieve, remember that the funeral for the loved one was a celebration of their life, not a loss. It signifies the life that your loved one lived, and you were privileged enough to be part of it.

Life will go on with or without you...

THE GOODBYE TO GRIEF

Hello Grief,

We met a while back when I least expected your arrival.

We bonded for the longest time.

You had become part of me and I had become part of you too.

Time has passed and you still at the same gloomy place.

I feel it's time for us to part ways.

I have since changed and you still the same as I met you back then. The partnership with

you is no longer working for me.

I have realized that you never change Grief

I am done throwing Pity Parties with you.

For that reason,

I am calling it quits......

Ciao!!

6

SELF HEALING

"*You will never know how strong you are until being strong is your only choice.*"
Bob Marley

Let me start off with a funny story about my eldest daughter, Rue. One day she was coming from holiday lessons to prepare for her 7th-grade examination. I never knew that my daughter was both a sprinter and high jumper, until this fateful day. As she was walking home, she passed through this street which had these two big vicious rottweilers. The gate to this house was always closed all the time as these dogs would eat you alive. On this fateful day, the gate was wide open. Unaware of her surroundings, Rue found herself walking past this open gate. Of course, this triggered some action from the two vicious dogs. Simultaneously, the mailman was also coming delivering mail from the opposite direction heading towards Rue. Upon hearing the loud bucks of those dogs, he turned to flee. In the meantime, Rue was also running for her dear life. You know when being strong remained her only option, she ran, and she found herself on the back of this fleeing mailman. This mailman just felt something land on his back gripping his neck for dear life. He could not shake her off and he ran with her on his back. Rue had exerted herself beyond her limits to save her life. When she reiterated her story, I laughed so bad my ribs hurt. Still to this day, I still laugh about this incident. This shows a lot of courage of how when you are pushed to your limits, you can do the unthinkable to save your life.

Thinking about it, the same applies to heal your wounds from your grief or divorce. Sometimes you must make drastic changes in your life for things to change for the better. Babying the grief might never work for some people. Making that big jump and surprising yourself will make changes happen in your life.

What is Healing to You?

There is a saying that goes, "When your cup is empty, you have nothing to share, but when your cup is overflowing then you have more than enough to spread around."

It means you should heal and live an abundant life for you to be able to love and be loved by other people.

- Healing is the real power to accept, recognize and acknowledge the pain and loss. Fighting back further hurts you. Don't allow yourself to be consumed by that pain.
- Healing is a continuous process that is never imposed on anyone. It is a personal choice, that requires work and dedication to follow through.
- Healing is about awareness of your negative emotions and recognizing that pain is temporary. It is also recognizing that the power to change your situation lies within you and no one else can do that for you.
- Healing is about allowing yourself to come to terms with your negativity and gathering the last little strength that might be left within you to move forward.
- Healing is a process that takes time and is never achieved by a quick fix. It requires patience on your part and being kind to yourself as you progress on this journey.
- Healing is a process that will teach you how to know yourself better and love yourself even more than before.
- Healing accepting the change in your life, reframing your thought process and helping you see the light at the end of the tunnel.

- Healing is about turning your pity party life into an exciting, happy, progressing, abundant life and a fresh start.
- Healing is about not attaching conditions to your happiness and freedom from pain. Stop saying, "I will start to heal when I find a new man, I will be happy when I can afford to go on a cruise." Be happy where you are, with what you have. What if you are never able to have money for that cruise? Are you going to be miserable for the rest of your life?
- Healing brings hope to the brokenhearted and to the bereaved.
- Healing is walking away from the self-defeating thoughts and self-destructive beliefs that will continue to sabotage your growth in life.
- Healing is using your pain to teach others what you learned from it.
- Healing is using the pain as a springboard to leap forward and higher in your life. It is letting your pain lubricate your joints so you move forward.

Healing starts in the mind. It's important to reframe your thoughts to reflect a positive mindset. Create a positive and conducive environment for healing. This will subsequently change your behaviors too. Healing never happens to people. It's the people that must get onto the healing journey. It's like when you want to get from point A to B. You must get onto some kind of transportation to get you where you want to go. You can't just wave a wand and magically get to your place, it's not a fairytale.

Going through all my predicaments, it dawned on me that I had to do something about my sad, grief-stricken and pity party state of mind. I had to quit wallowing in my pain and expecting it to just disappear one day. I learned that healing is accepting, dealing with my pain and learn to move past it or learn to live with it. The choice was mine to make. I had to come to terms with my pain and realize that I was stuck in this, "poor me," mindset and it had not fixed my pain, not one bit. How long was I going to live like this? This grief-stricken life had taken a toll on me more than I could handle.

All this realization happened when I attended the International Women of Virtue Conference. I heard other women sharing their stories about their struggles and how they managed to overcome them and moved on. I felt I could identify with this group. There was a preacher from Edmonton, Jessie, who preached about being that "Certain Woman," from Judges 9:53.

It talks about a certain woman who threw an upper millstone upon Abimelech's head and crushed his skull. This guy Abimelech was going to kill many people who were fleeing from him. They thought they were safe until he was able to break down the gates of their hiding place. That "certain woman" waited for the right moment and dropped that stone to crush his head. I felt inspired by this. I thought I could be that "certain woman", who was going to crush my pain and my grief on the head to stop it from following me everywhere I went.

I prayed about getting the strength to lift that heavy burden in my heart. Do you know, God works in wonderful ways? I felt that heavy burden being lifted off my shoulders that weekend. I knew this was the beginning of my healing journey. I knew I had to do most of the work to get onto the healing journey myself. This was a big step in my life. That day I broke down and I cried openly about my pain and my losses. I had had so many losses and defeats in my life and in my relationships and I had had enough of that roller coaster life. There is a saying which goes, "You attract who you are," I was in pain for the longest while and I needed to be free of that junk and start a new life!

It was after I started the healing journey that I realized how broken I had been. I had been toxic to many people and I had been living this negative life in which I never thought anything good could happen to me. I used to wonder why I was so stuck in that negative mindset. Now I knew this was all because I was hanging around the same limited minded people that had no wish to find happiness nor to change their "sorry lives."

Looking back, I had no idea how I even managed to survive that long? That was a boring and painful life I tell you!!

Rediscover your "why"

I still did not understand how much time I needed to heal and move on without this cloud of pain lingering over my head. Looking back at the time I wallowed in my grief and pain, my children and my family had stuck by me. My mother would tell me that it will be over soon and I should just give myself time.

I finally re-discovered **my "why?"** It was rooted in my love for my children who needed me most and were looking up to me to help them through their struggles. I had myself too. I still have a long life ahead of me that still needs to be discovered. My children still needed a solid parental figure in their lives to help them steer towards success and prosperity. I asked myself, "How could I support my children fully when I couldn't even help myself." I need to heal so that I could be there a hundred per cent for them. My children had grown without a solid male figure in their lives and I learned that it could affect their relationships with the opposite sex too. I had to get my act together, get onto the healing journey and be fully present when they needed me the most.

You know when you have been looking at life through a biased lens, everything looks dark and stuck. I had to look from inside out and saw that I had a lot of unforgiveness going on in my life. I had hurt some people and I had been hurt by so many people. I had also lost so many loved ones. That pain had closed my heart to healing. I had been walking around with all this junk in my heart. Some people saw it, but most of the people were unaware I had this cloud following me around.

After that women conference, I talked to some ladies from Montreal. One had gone through a rough divorce and the other had lost her husband many years back and was still bitter at how her in-laws had treated her. She felt she had to get justice done and believed the in-laws owed her an apology. I asked her one question that got her thinking. I asked her, "What if the in-laws never apologize to you? Are you going to hold your healing and your happiness hostage for the rest of your life, while they are living theirs?" She looked at me as if to say, "that makes sense."

She told me that she had never thought of it that way. All this time she felt that one day these in-laws would come and apologize to her for hurting her. I reminded her that they had lost their loved one too and they probably expected her to apologize to them. Sometimes it takes a few words from a stranger to open your heart and mind to see reality.

After you have been grieving for some time, you need to check if anything in your life has changed for the better. Some people will wallow in their grief and throw all these fancy pity parties so that they can get the attention they miss from their spouses. Look at the length of time you have been stuck in that wallowing state. Is that the life you want for yourself and your children, family, and friends? How has this affected your health and your interactions with other people and your relationships in general? Holding onto your grief forever will create anger, negativity, and insecurity in your life. Your relationships will suffer because of this. You lose your joy, and this will end up throwing you into a space of loneliness and the next thing, mental health issues find their way to you. You would have created the environment conducive to such.

Now ask yourself what is your "why?" It might be different from mine.

- This must be something that motivates you to jump on the healing journey and never look back?
- It must be something that will improve your life tomorrow.
- It must be something that helps you first, then your whole family?

"We do not see things as they are, but we see them as we are."
By Anais Nin

I saw the world as broken and wounded as I was before I healed. When you heal, you do not bleed on everyone around you even those that are trying to help you. Protect everyone around you from your bleeding heart. It's not fair to them. You have a different version of the world.

In order to heal properly here are some steps to find healing. Everyone is different and healing time is different with everyone. So, follow these steps and see healing coming your way.

16 steps to finding healing

1. Start by forgiving yourself. There could be times when you continue to bash yourself about the things that you did or allowed to be done that you now see as having caused barriers to your healing process. Forgiving yourself will then open doors for you to forgive others.

2. You need to give yourself time to heal. Do you feel like you are under pressure to heal, in order to impress other people? This is for you and you are doing it for you, then other people will follow. It's not a quick fix neither is it DIY. You need to make sure that you are aware of what is going on during this healing process so that when you happen to fall off the wagon, you will remember where to start.

3. Look at your childhood, are there somethings that pop out that have repeated themselves in your present-day life? Are there things that you were meant to believe that you see now as being barriers to your progress? Those childhood memories can create huge barriers to your healing process as you might believe that that's the way things should be. This could be abuse, ranging from sexual, physical, verbal, financial and psychological abuses. The parental influence that was in your home growing up can be another contributing factor.

4. Do you have any feelings of abandonment that you have not dealt with? This could be in your previous relationships or with your ex or the late spouse? You might feel like the death of your spouse was like abandonment to you. You need to deal with these feelings so that you understand that their time was up, and they needed to cross over. I felt like my husband had abandoned me and the kids when he passed away. I had to come to terms with his death and let go.

5. Some of you might have gone through some serious traumatic experiences, with the ending of previous relationships. You might have this strong feeling that history will repeat itself and you go through the same trauma again. You could develop this idea that this is how life is lived. In order to heal and move forward, you need to repeat your "why?" As well as replace these negative thoughts with more positive

thoughts. I know it's easier said than done, but changes start in your mindset and the rest will follow. In order to heal in this case, you need to reframe your mindset, start creating what you really want and then start to verbalize it. Doing this will diminish the presence of fear and anxiety in your life.

6. All emotional hurts and pains need to be dealt with by facing the pain head-on. Let yourself feel, experience and go through the pain. That way you will not have any repressed and suppressed feelings that might resurface in the future. Emotional baggage is very sneaky. It can sneak up on you when you are least prepared for it. This comes in the form of snapping at people for no reason or one small issue can be blown of out proportion. Letting the pain run its course will curb the recurrence of the same pain. You will be aware of the triggers and can do something preventative to stop it from recurring and progressing.

7. Healing your emotions is key to the whole healing process as all the trauma is locked up in your emotions. That's the reason that emotional healing needs to be dissected fully and dealt with piece by piece to make sure no emotional baggage remains unsolved. I cannot stress this enough. This needs to be looked at thoroughly as a lot of people just scan the top and forget about the issues of yesteryear.

8. If you cannot deal with the pain alone, then get professional help through a coach, counselor, or your doctor can make a referral to a psychiatrist or psychologist.

9. Sometimes our beliefs can hold us hostage. Some cultures can be detrimental to your healing process. Find out what your culture says about the healing ways and processes. Look at your inner self. Do they work for you or not? You might have been in a different culture and then you move to another part of the world where everything is done differently. I also went through language shock, culture shock, food shock, driving shock, as people drive on the wrong side of the road according to where I grew up. All these need to be taken into consideration and dealt with individually.

10. Being open to change can also open your eyes to see many ways to help

you start your healing process.

11. When you start the healing process forgive those that have wronged you, and never expect anyone of them to send you an apology for any reason. They might not have any idea they hurt you, or what challenges you are going through. Even if they know what you are going through, they might want you to apologize to them. You must also realize that they are hurting just like you.

12. Seeking revenge is just prolonging the healing process. It will just create more bitterness and frustrations from both sides. Just let it go. Don't be a dumb widow who seeks revenge. Just let it go, no matter what it is.

13. Nowadays there are coaches that are available on a one-on-one basis and in groups as well. Help is available and you can heal and move on.

14. Educate your mind. Surround yourself with useful people and resources that are helpful in your predicament. Be mindful of some people who come into your life when you are most vulnerable. They might suck the life out of you.

15. You must be committed to the process and love to be on the healing journey. Otherwise, it's going to be like a chore and will not be effective at all. The healing process will come with its own challenges. It's the same as you are recovering from addictions. You will need people around you that will cheer you on or hold you accountable, like a coach or an accountability partner, or your pastor or an unbiased friend. These people will make sure that if you fall off the wagon you will be held responsible. This will help you to get up and continue with the healing process.

16. Hang out with like-minded people that you see making great progress in their lives, so you can learn from them. My late friend Enid said to me one day, "Don't let the death of your husband claim another life, yours." This made me realize that I had to turn my life around and get on the healing process.

The Healing Prayer

Prayer can help you to heal and start a new happy life. This prayer helped me, it might help you as well, if not you can create what works for you.

"I deserve to heal from this pain.
  I deserve to love and to be loved again.
  I am worthy of love.
  I am very beautiful and strong. This grief has made me
  Stronger.
  I will take care of myself, my children and give the best I can.
  I am ready to turn this ship around to the land of peace, happiness and
most of all love.
  I love myself more now and I will what I can to remain true to myself.
  All negativity and bitterness that have been following me, I release you
today.
  I am a new person and I am ready to move on without you.
  So Good Bye pain,
  I never want to see you again."

Healing Therapies

Healing using the practice of harm reduction is becoming very common, although most people still don't understand this process. I am sure now you are thinking I am going to write about drugs and addiction treatment? No!

Practicing harm reduction in your life is the ability to know your own power over your adversities. Harm reduction is looking for solutions to problems and challenges instead of taking a quick fix. This process is a very useful discipline that will keep you on track to achieve a happy and prosperous life that is free of all the past pains that might have plagued your life before. Harm reduction is also about being kind to your mind, body, and soul.

- Drinking habits - how much alcohol do you take? Are you taking alcohol as a quick fix to your pain? Does the pain go away when you are sober again or the pain resurfaces again? The drinking is not going to fix your problems and heal your pain. Look at what other coping skills you can learn instead of using alcohol to get temporary relief. Were you drowning your sorrows in alcohol hoping to erase the pain? If so, you probably discovered that it does not work that way.

- Healthy eating- What are you feeding your body with? Junk Food? You might say, "Rose I do not have enough money to buy proper food." Yes, I understand that money could be an issue, but there are ways around this. Look for a community kitchen in your area where they teach people how to make thrifty meals for free. You will get to keep the food and load your freezer. When you eat healthily, you develop a healthy mind and a healthy body too. Drink more water to keep yourself hydrated. Your body needs fluids to flush out toxins in your body. Remember that when you want to grab a pop instead of a glass of water. 8 glasses of water daily are the minimum a person should drink per day.

- Start to look at life from a different perspective. Instead of pulling through life, aim to thrive.

- Harm Reduction is about getting rid of the negative mindset and behaviors, replacing them with positive thinking and kind behaviors. Being negative and not healing properly has not done me any good. It only hurt me more. Positive thinking and positive behaviors will attract more positive energy towards you and that will get the universe, the Law of Attraction, to work with you. When you are a joyful person you also attract like-minded people to you. Scrap the pity party mindset for good and move into joyous life.

- Harm Reduction in Relationships - This is a huge one. This could be with family, yourself, your kids and work. When you do not look for faults in people, you live a better life. Learn not to worry about the little things in life and learn to let go of things that don't really matter in life. Stop being too analytical about life as this will get you nowhere. Trust me, you should rather choose your battles and turn a blind eye, than worry and fight certain battles. This will remove any bitterness and resentment that might have built up over time blocking your healing process. Most relationships are built on emotional responses. If you still have a truck full of emotional baggage that you are carrying around, then that is going to affect your relationships with everyone including yourself. Emotional baggage does not go away with an easy fix. It requires you to start from inside out and look through all the issues that you have gone through from childhood.

• You also need to express those feelings that continue to haunt you. This is also another way of harm reduction to yourself. You become aware of what the hidden emotions are. Then you will let them run their course and deal with them by finding ways to heal. That way this prevents any recurring of the same issues later or from a different angle.

Writing/Journaling for Healing

Begin by asking yourself some of these questions:

• What is keeping you up at night?
• What is frustrating you the most about your life?
• Did the passing of your husband hurt you that you could not talk about it?
• You felt it better to hide the feeling so you can keep up with your daily chores and life?
• Is it any of your friends, family members including the in-laws that hurt you?

Writing or Journaling is also another recognized effective healing therapy to heal from trauma. I used it and it helped me to release all the suppressed emotions from way back. Your brain believes what you tell it to do, so when you write all the hurts and frustrations, you are telling your brain to remove those hurts from your mind onto a piece of paper. This will free your cluttered mind from carrying all that baggage onto the piece of paper. Writing will help you to express your deepest feelings. Those feelings that you could not express face to face even to the one that hurt you will find expression. It releases these unbiased feelings as sometimes talking to people might be awkward or scary to do. It frees your soul and unblocks any blockages that might have been an impediment to your healing process.

Writing is therapeutic in that as you write you can have time to reflect on what you wrote and see how you feel when you read it back afterward. Do not make a mistake of reading it back while the thoughts and memories are still flowing as you are writing them. Read it back once you are done the writing. You also review it to see if what is on paper is all that has been hurting you. All those feelings that had been stuck can be accessed when you start writing to heal, as it opens your subconscious mind. Just let those feelings flow and watch the magic of therapeutic writing work. Once you are done the writing you will be surprised how much weight is lifted off your shoulders.

For widows, you can write anything that caused you grief from when your husband was still alive, your childhood years, single years and so on. This also could be anything that was exacerbated by family members from both your in-laws and your side of the family. Your kids could have contributed to this as well, even the late husband might have done quite a few things to hurt you and you might have never looked at how it made you feel until now. It could also be the events surrounding the death of your spouse, which you could not share with anyone. You can now share it with this piece of paper. It's like you are renting out to a good listener who is none judgmental and yet it lets you release all the pain and frustrations quietly.

If you have suffered **a relationship breakdown** or a divorce you can also use this form of healing therapy. This list might contain who wronged you, how many times, where they wronged you, the date and maybe the time. People can be that detailed.

In this case, do everything the same but, you list down the names of all the individuals that you got emotionally involved with, got attached to, had a relationship with and later caused you grief. Your Ex could be on the top of the list, this is totally fine. Write the list of the names and their hurts as follows: -

NAME

John

NEGATIVE QUALITIES

He was controlling,

Very short tempered,

He was financially abusive,

Disrespectful.

NAME

Peter

NEGATIVE QUALITIES

Financially abusive,

Controlling,

Insecure

Next step, look at the lists and see if there are any repeats in the qualities of individuals that hurt you. Highlight all the qualities that are common on your list. Why do you think that you keep attracting the same bad people? This will tell you a lot about you. It tells you how much healing you need to go through and the areas that need to be addressed. If you continue to attract people that are controlling, it means growing up you have been exposed to this behavior from your parents, school or with some of your siblings. Most of this will emanate from the parental influence you had growing up. You can also redo this exercise if you feel you did not write to everyone who hurt you.

This process is very transformational as it works wonders psychologically. After you have written your list, upon reflecting it, you can feel the difference in your emotions. The writing process will help you to make peace with your terrible past without anyone judging you. Sometimes you cannot share what really happened to you when you got hurt due to various reasons known to you and your spouse.

If this process is done correctly, the brain is tricked into thinking that all that garbage has been disposed of out of the brain. The brain will then deactivate that trauma and will redefine it with joy and happiness. In order to create healing or change, you remove the hurts, the pain and fill up the void with something positive.

Another way of writing to heal would be to write a letter either to everyone who hurt you or you write it to yourself. I used this process also. I wrote a letter to myself telling myself how much I was hurting and what that damage had caused in my life since the passing of my husband. I also wrote about the relationships that had brought more grief to my already battered heart. It helped me to release all the hidden and forgotten frustrations and pain that I thought I had dealt with. The journaling process helped me to open the doors to my soul that had been suppressed for too long.

Making Collages

For this exercise, you will need lots of magazines, newspapers, pairs of scissors, plain paper, paper glue, and crayons. I know you wondering what I am trying to teach you.

This is another way of releasing negative emotions from every cell of your body to pictures, and images that you will stick onto a piece of paper. This will take you back to your childhood for a few minutes.

- Think about what you want to portray in the collage? How can you show what is hurting you the most in the form of an image or picture? You can draw it or cut it out from the magazines.
- Once you know what it is you want to portray, then cut off the pictures and the words you want to use. Use these to tell your story and see the magic of making collages work again for you!!
- If you cannot find the right pictures you can also use your own photos.

Once you complete your story then ask yourself the following questions:

1. How difficult was it to come up with your story?
2. What about finding pictures and words to describe your story?

3. What emotions were triggered?
4. How did you deal with those emotions?
5. What does your story in the collage say about the gravity of your pain?
6. Did you feel that it helped to bring up all the emotions?
7. Is there anything you think you missed out?

You can also repeat this process later if you feel that you need to heal further. This will also help you to vent on paper which is not judgmental.

Using the Focus Method

"Where focus goes, energy flows. Where energy flows, whatever you're focusing on grows. Shift your focus toward where you want to go, and your actions will take you in that direction."
Tony Robbins

FOCUS

I learned the meaning of this acronym from Pastor Trina Patterson.

- F—figuring out the problem
- O—observing and obeying
- C—confronting the pain and conquering it
- U—understanding and using what you must heal
- S—stand firm with your choices and decisions and remain respectful to yourself.

Your life after losing your spouse or going through a divorce could have been put out of focus. You will need to do some calibrating of your life, so you can recharge your batteries to refocus.

F- After you return from the funeral, reality hits. You are alone in the house and are in utter dismay of reality! At this stage, do not try to fix anything yet. You must really figure out what you want to do moving forward. Look at the issues on hand, the Widows Tasks or Divorcee to-do list. Figure out your desired outcome and look at how your beliefs are going to impact your plans. What did your mama tell you to do or not to do growing up? These will have a huge impact on your beliefs.

O- Observe and Obey. Look at where your attitudes, thoughts, and behaviors are coming from. Are you making big decisions out of ignorance or fear? Be open to receiving advice from others that have walked that same road or what God is telling you if you are a believer. If not listen to your gut ladies!

C- Confront and conquer. It's time to confront your fears, pain or problems. Now that you are single, crying and wallowing in your grief is not going to change the situation. You have been pushed into a corner with your problems or pain with your back against the wall, and with nowhere to run. What are you going to do? Give up? Really? It's time to fight back and repossess your power back. Believe in yourself and you will conquer.

U- Use what is available to you. Understand the things you can change and those that you don't have control over then let it be. You are now the master of your own destiny. Healing starts with the knowledge and belief that you must defeat the Goliaths that come your way. Change only occurs when you understand the need to make it happen.

S- Standing firm on your promise is key to moving forward. When you want to go on a healing journey, staying steadfast in that decision will help you achieve your goals of healing. Respect your decisions and remember those decisions will affect other people like your families, your children even yourself.

Meditation or Focus

When you are going through trauma from grieving or divorce focusing is a huge challenge to be achieved. During my grieving process, I had issues with keeping my mind focused. The worst time was soon after the funeral. Your brain is so scattered and running faster than lightning. Your head feels like you have a dozen spinning heads on your neck with thoughts running wild. This life-changing trauma has caused your mind to go into a sudden search mode to find solutions. This is normal, very few people can focus during this difficult time. I used to get so absent-minded that people would talk to me and I would not hear a word of what they were saying to me. I could see their lips move though, but no sound came through to me. I had times when I slipped into my grieving mode and shut everything out.

This mental state is supposed to be manageable without therapy or medications as it is sometimes temporary. If it gets worse to a point that it affects your daily living, then seek professional help. People are different and handle trauma differently too.

Focus Tools

1. Meditation and Visualization

Meditation is the best tool to help you to regroup your thoughts. It helps to slow down your thought process and helps your brain to recharge. Meditation also helps to remove any negative energy around you. Research says every day our brain goes through a gazillion thoughts a day. 95% of all this information is garbage and toxic. Which means that only 5% of that information is useful. So, it means that the brain is working 24/7. So, imagine what happens when your life is hit by a traumatic event when you cannot focus don't beat yourself up, it's just a wave that will pass. I use the "OM—OM," for my meditation exercises. You can also find more on YouTube videos.

Visualization on the same token helps to refocus your brain as well. It works by you forming a picture in your mind, then focusing on that image in your mind. In your mind, start to work out how you can have that goal or image manifest into reality by compartmentalizing your thoughts. It's like you put your thoughts in a box and wait for them to manifest. This will allow you to move away from those thoughts for a while and work on some new ones. This act of boxing the information declutters your clouded mind. It also helps to remove the clutter from your mind onto the paper.

1. Have a to-do list that you follow so you don't overlook anything. I used to tell my kids to remind me about the important tasks that I needed to do. They were very good at jolting my mind. This will also help them to be part of the healing process and as they feel they are doing something to help you feel better.

2. Assign or delegate to some trusted people so that they carry out some tasks for you if they get overwhelming for you. Let people around you know that you are struggling with remembering or focusing on things and they too will assist you. Be careful who you tell though, as other people can take advantage of this weakness in you. Help is everywhere but be mindful whom to ask for it.

3. Be kind to yourself. You have gone through a wringer and need to take care of yourself. This can take some time to get back to normal and refocus.

4. Take some time off to recharge and clear your mind. Go to the gym to burn all the stress away. Sometimes taking a power nap for 30 – 60 minutes helps you to refocus and rejuvenate your brain. Be careful not to oversleep!

Fear of The Unknown

Do not let fear pull you down, as Fear itself has no idea how much strength you have. (Unknown)

Dealing with a fear of the unknown can be another big hurdle to get over. You had been used to being on a certain routine and now things have suddenly changed. Fear can also hold you back as it feels like you are walking in the dark and not seeing your feet! Have you ever walked in the dark and don't see where you are placing your feet? That's scary for me! Fear can also paralyze you and if you are not careful you can be stuck in that zone where you don't want to try new things. Giving up on your dreams and yourself might seem to be the easy way out, but is that what you really want for yourself?

Fear also makes you shy away from people as you have no confidence to face the world once you are alone.

Fear can also make you doubt yourself even in the things that you used to do as sometimes you lose trust in yourself. The fear of being a single parent to three children. Fear to continue teaching at the same College where we both worked, scared me. I was triggered many times, but the staff members helped me to deal with this every time I broke down. After the funeral, at a College Assembly, the MC asked for a moment of silence for my late Husband. Later he asked me to say a few words. I felt stuck to my chair; I was scared. I could not walk to the stage. I felt I was going to trip and fall. I only got some courage when people started clapping for me. When I got to the stage I only managed to say, "Thank you, everyone, for the support you gave my children, my family and myself." After that, I was sobbing uncontrollably.

My heart goes to you if you are still fresh in the widowhood journey. It's hard and scary, but it's doable. You will feel lost in this world but don't worry you will find yourself. You will be scared to walk on the street as those people you know will look at you as if you have this big misery banner stuck to your forehead. After a while, you will get used to it and soon you will be walking with your head held high.

When you decide to get back into the dating world, Mr. Fear will be right there to terrorize you again. I will share with you some steps to follow to calm that fear later in the book. I know if you have been hurt, rejected and heartbroken, your biggest fear is that the next guy will do the same to you and repeat the cycle. Do not stress over this issue. You will regain your groove, and be a love magnet again.

After some time, I found that fear is always meant to be there, but it was up to me, how I was going to deal with it. Was I going to let it steal my joy and keep me hostage? I decided that enough was enough. I had had it with fear. It was time to move forward with my life.

The other fears were caused by financial status. From two incomes down to one income. It was going to take some time before all the other benefits were going to be released. We lived in a big house that needed to be maintained and bills still came in. Most of the money had been invested in an engineering business that had not taken off. That was another thorn in my flesh. How was I going to settle these things?

On second thoughts, fear can also be good in that it can push you out of your comfort zone. Remember the story I told you about my daughter clinging onto the back of the mailman? Fear made her jump with everything she had.

Looking at other superstars like Tina Turner, if she had let fear encompass her life, she would not have achieved what she is today. She took the bull by the horns and left with nothing to her name. Look at her today! She is my inspiration, every time I want to give up, I will ask myself, "What would Tina do in this situation?" Who is your role model? what do you learn from this individual that helps you to hang on when times are tough or when fear stares right into your eyes?

Get Rid of Fear

Hello Fear,

You have had the best of me for a while now.

You consumed every cell in my body.

I let you control my life for too long.

I have had enough of you controlling my life, my happiness, and my freedom.

I am ready to slam the door shut right into your face and close you out of my life.

I have since found out that you are a toothless dog and you will not have that grip over my life anymore.

You and I do not belong together anymore.

I have grown to be a strong woman and will not let you in the way of my healing and success.

I am free at last of your jaws.

Go on your way FEAR,

Don't look back

I will not join you ever!!!

Your name

Keep this prayer handy and when fear comes back to read it, helped me a lot.

Mantras

Here is a small mantra I want you to write and stick where you can read it daily.

This pain or trauma will not hurt me ever again.

Pain, you will not continue to gain space in my mind and body anymore.

effective NOW,

TODAY,

I am going to raise the rent of the space in my mind so,

I can kick you out of my life completely.

I know you cannot afford the new rent as it will continue to increase every time you try to

catch up on your arrears.

I am above you, pain.

Self-Talk for Healing

Self-talk is the art of speaking with yourself, but at the same time letting your brain hear it. Those words will stick to your subconscious mind. This, in turn, will affect your everyday thoughts. Self-talk can be both positive and negative. I am sure there are sometimes when you do certain things without thinking or paying attention. Later, you will say to yourself, "What was I thinking?" It's because your mind was busy listening to your self-talk or it got stuck on your previous self-talk conversation.

Look at how much time you spend on self-talk?

What is the topic of your self-talk?

Are you going to give in to overthinking?

This usually happens when you get stuck overthinking about a certain negative topic during your self-talk, especially when your mind is idle and unproductive. This repeated conversation does not bring any solutions, it's just the **poor me talk** that does not get you anywhere.

Self-talk started when you were a kid, remember when you used to hold a full conversation with no one else, but yourself? Sometimes you could have your toys around. Whatever belief or environment you grew up in, can affect your self-talk later in life.

Some people use self-talk to fight fear, self-doubt and encourage themselves. It affects their behaviors and moods. **Ever told yourself, "You can do this?" I know I have. It has helped to do things that I would have backed out of.**

8 Tips to Change Your Negative Self-Talk

Look at what is causing you grief or frustration.

Can you change or control it?

Can you change the behavior of the person who caused you the pain?

If not, then don't stress over it. I was tired of being a volunteer victim of my thoughts.

So, I decided to do something about it.

1. Start telling your mind to listen to the word "STOP." When you start thinking about anything negative, tell yourself to, "STOP." This will remind you to refocus on your self-talk.

2. Rubber band snaps: When you start negative self-talking, just snap on the rubber band as a reminder that the self-talk is unproductive. The pain from the rubber band, will jolt your mind and stop the negative self-talk.

3. Journaling and writing. This will also free your flustered mind and it improves your self-talk as you will get more focused.

4. Replace the self-limiting self-talk with questions. This is a very useful way to use self-talk. For example, the self-talk will tell you that, "You cannot recover from the widowhood trauma." You would respond with a question like, "Am I the first one to lose a husband? If not then, I will do it just like the others have done it." Usually, it's the negative response that wants to come first but take a deep breath and respond.

5. Stop using the word, "Hate" in your conversations. Using the expression creates an environment conducive to negativity. Change that word to "dislike." Its softer on the ears and your tongue too. We say this word when we are mad over something.

6. Have you ever noticed how much self-talk we do to ourselves? I watched a movie by Taraj P. Henson called, "**What Men Want?**" The protagonist could hear what people were saying to themselves. Imagine the horrific conversations she heard. Oh my God! I laughed all the way to the end of that movie. Even some much-respected people in that movie would say some absurd stuff to themselves. Imagine what you say sometimes? What we must remember is that we are not our thoughts. Rather, we have control over what we think and say in our self-talk conversations.

7. From time to time be mindful of your thoughts. What you spend most of your time thinking and self-talking on affects your daily living. Sometimes we spend lots of time-solving a situation before it becomes a problem. This will create lots of anxiety and worry and all for nothing. **"Dhololo."** (nothing).

8. Stop body shaming. This is the negative self-talk that is done when you dislike your body image. "Oh, I hate these legs. Oh, my boobs are too small," As women, we are never satisfied with what God gave us at birth. So now since you're widowed, you look at yourself in the mirror and you tell yourself that no one will love you again because you are ugly, or because you are too big. When you look at yourself in the mirror and you don't like what you see, ask yourself how can you change it? If you don't like what you see, then change it, you are not a tree that's stuck in one place. If you think your lips are too thin, then remember people are paying money to get them fuller, then do that, if you can't afford it then find other ways. I have heard some girls use bottles to vacuum their lips and they swell. There is always something that can be done to improve your body, instead of body shaming yourself. I call this self-destructive behavior.

The Positive Self-Talk to Your Body

Hello, Body,

You got me the man that took me to the altar the very first time.

Now I am called Mrs.——because he saw positive things in me and loved me.

Body, you also carried my children, and now I am called mommy because of you and God.

You are with me everywhere I go.

You are my best buddy and you are my life.

I apologize for being ungrateful before, but now I going to love you and take care of you.

Body, we are a team.

Lots of love

Your name.......

Benefits of Positive Self-Talk

- Positive self-talk is a powerful tool to increase your self-confidence and self-esteem when you feel bogged down by situations or people.
- It helps you see the world from a different lens.
- Self-talk can also help us to react to things and situations mindfully.
- Self-talk can change your perspective about a problem that you are facing.

Safety and Awareness

Safety:

In order to heal your body and mind, you need to create a safe place and a peaceful environment. Our minds and bodies need these to feel safe in order to heal. Your mind needs to be safe so that it can tell the body to relax and heal. That way the body does not go into the "fighter and flight mode." This requires you to be honest and true to yourself as well. The worst that can happen to you is to compare yourself to other people who far are better than you. When you do compare yourself, then strive to improve yourself instead of just wishing and then doing nothing about it.

Awareness:

When you finally become aware that something is wrong with your situation you might be stuck in that situation already. That's the time you need to start changing the situation.

This could also apply to failed relationships. Maybe you keep attracting the same bozos, who come to waste your time, and who dump you like they never had a good time with you before. Are you still facing the same triggers repeatedly? It means you need healing in that area so that those triggers do not have an effect on you anymore.

7

DO WIDOWS NEED TO FORGIVE TOO?

What is forgiveness?

Forgiveness to me is accepting my past as it is. It's about being able to live with my past and to move on into the next chapter of my life. It's about using my pain as a stepping board to sprint forward. I have learned that the best revenge for those who hurt you, is to rise above the pain and succeed.

Forgiveness is a process like healing. It's being at peace with your past and the world. It's a process of letting go of what other people have wronged you and sometimes without even telling them that you have forgiven them. It is a long process that needs time and not a quick fix. You can skip a meal but never skip forgiveness. It is the key to the healing journey.

Forgiveness is setting yourself free from the burden of carrying all that bitterness and resentment that was created when you were hurt. When you give and receive forgiveness, you are free of that bondage, and you take your power back from that situation. Continuing to hold onto that bitterness and anger will set you up for failure in the long run. Unforgiveness is like a time bomb waiting to explode. One small trigger and it's like a volcano.

Forgiveness is getting rid of that heavy load of resentment off your shoulders. It does not mean that what happened to you was right or not hurtful. NO! By showing your unforgiveness, it means that whoever hurt you can still control your happiness and emotions. The perpetrator can still do more things to hurt you because they know how to get to you. Forgiving them shows them that what they did cannot control you anymore. Now I say it is a way *to confuse the devil in his tracks.*

Before you forgive everyone else, start by forgiving yourself first. This gives you the strength to forgive other people that hurt you. Tell yourself that you are forgiven for letting yourself down and allowing what other people did to you to take your power away from you. Forgiving yourself gets you the power to look from inside out and letting go of all the negative emotions. Allow yourself to deal with the present, accept it and then let go of the past. This will give you the strength to love and accept yourself as God's own creation.

I had to go through the process of forgiving my husband because in my mind he had abandoned me and his children. I was very angry with him for not fighting to be alive. I had to forgive my in-laws as I felt they did not give me the support that I needed. But now I see that they were also going through the loss of a loved one too. They were probably expecting more support from me while I was expecting the same from them.

The Serenity Prayer helped me a lot in order to be able to forgive and continue my healing process. It made me understand that I cannot control how people think and behave. Neither can I control the world that we live in. I got to know that I had no control over what happened when my husband passed away and I could not control how people treated me afterward. The only thing I could control was myself and how I am going to carry on with my life and my children. Now I am at peace with my husband's passing.

Serenity Prayer

Lord grant me the
  Serenity
  To Accept
  The things I cannot change
  The "Courage to change the things I can"
  And
  "Wisdom"
  To know the difference.

To this day, whenever I feel overwhelmed or frustrated with situations, I go back to the Serenity Prayer. It became my source of strength, and it made me accept people for who they are. This prayer became the turning point for me. What is your turning point right now?

Steps to Achieving Forgiveness

I love this quote by Sylvester Stallone when he said to his son. He said, **"Son don't even do them as they did you. Just disappear and do better. That's the best revenge."**

It makes me realize that when someone hurts you, revenge will not change anything for both you and them. Rising above those people that hurt you gives you more power over them. It's normal to have scars that remind you of the hurt or the pain you suffered. Some scars are not visible, but they are in our hearts, thoughts, and emotions. It's left to the individual to know how they will react to those scars. That's where forgiveness starts.

The process of forgiveness starts by looking at the scars and asking yourself, how long am I going to hold onto these scars? How has holding onto the pain and bitterness from those scars changed your life for the better? I know having gone through widowhood, the scars gave me some comfort and ownership. The pain you feel after losing a loved one could be the only thing that makes you feel like you are still close to them. But is that true? Truthfully speaking holding onto the baggage is like overloading your already overloaded mind with stuff. When you forgive you let all that baggage go and you feel much better afterward.

Step 1 Reconnect with Your Spiritual Being

Turn your cares or burdens onto the Lord. Sometimes you need help to forgive some people in your life. Forgiveness can be hard and challenging. We are not Jesus who forgave people just like that. Sometimes it just cannot happen. Asking for help from the Lord will be your way out to forgive people and their baggage.

Step 2 Don't Hit the Sack Angry, It's A Bad Idea.

This habit is very common among humans. Me included. I realized asking God to help me release that anger helped me deal with the anger in a more productive way, instead of lashing out at people. When you go to bed angry this causes restless nights and sometimes nightmares. Figure out what caused the frustrations. Is it something I can control or not? If I can control it then I should do something about it, like talking to whoever hurt me, in a calm voice, and tone to see if they understand where I am coming from. If I cannot talk to whoever hurt me, then I find ways to deal with it. I found out that approaching someone who hurt you while your emotions are high is like putting more gasoline into an already raging fire. Take a deep breath or remove yourself from the situation until you calm down. What you must bear in mind is that those people that thrive in hurting people are broken and wounded themselves. The sad thing is, they want to bring more people around them, and so they can share and spread their brokenness. When you remember this, you will be mindful never to engage in some power struggles.

Step 3 Let Bygones Be Bygones

The past should never be relived. What good does it bring to you to continue torturing yourself with what so and so did to you some time back? It makes us relive the pain again. If there are still triggers like a ringing tone that still brings bad memories, then you need healing for sure. It took me a long time for me to get over the sound of the phone call late at night that accompanied the news that Temba had passed away. For a while, when the house phone rang after 9.00 pm my heart would skip a beat. I would be thinking who else is dead again? Sometimes we must see if it's worth it to keep reliving the hurts or just let it go and move on?

Step 4 Stop Blame Shifting

I like what Dr Wayne W. Dyer said. *"Whenever you are upset over what people have said or done to you. Allow yourself to feel the pain without blaming who caused it."*

Then tell yourself that no one has the power to make you feel uneasy without your consent and that you are not willing to grant authority to anyone right now. Tell yourself that you will take the responsibility of how you choose to react or feel. Remember that when people hurt you, their acts are registered with Karma. Karma will never forget their address no matter what. This should be your consolation.

Step 5 Take Responsibility for Your Actions

If you are in the wrong, please be reasonable and take responsibility for your actions. Sometimes while you are going through the **Widowhood** journey you can also hurt some people in the process. You might be trying to seek revenge for what was done to you sometime back. Do not expect people to make you exempt from that simply because you are a widow. Don't hurt people and pretend like it's a cry for help because you have some emotional issues going on. Be an adult and fix it.

Step 6 Be Like A River That Flows

"When you give up interfering and opt instead to stream like water-gently, softly and unobtrusively – you become forgiveness itself."

Dr Wayne Dyer.

Be like a river and allow yourself to go deep into your heart and let the water take away the hurts. As the river continues to flow let it take away all the pain to the ocean. Let it go and see how easy life becomes. Learn not to stress too much over life's ups and downs. Life is too short to seek revenge over people that hurt you. If you do that, then you are lowering yourself to their levels. Be like an eagle that never hangs around chickens. Chickens will never be like the eagle. The eagle can soar higher, above, and beyond where the enemy will never reach. Remember you are better than those people that try to inflict pain on you. Life will strike you in the face, but if you can still shake your head, you know you can still get up and go on.

Step 7 Don't Try to Control People and Their Minds

Remember in life that people are different. So never try to change people to think and behave as you do. People will change when they are ready to change when their time is right for them, not for you. Remember that even when grieving, people grieve differently, including your children. My son Ronnie always told me to let be people be who they are. He really has understood this principle that people will never change for you. Do not always try to have the last word in every conversation or argument. Don't try to be heard all the time. Let people feel your presence.

"People will forget what you told them, but they will never forget how you made them feel."
   Dr Maya Angelo

Do not let your ego control you. Be a good listener and be slow to react.

When you do this, it's easy to walk away from pain and hurtful people.

Step 8 Do Not Keep A Laundry List of Your Pains

It's like you are reliving the pain repeatedly. Sometimes, those people that wronged have you have no idea that you are keeping track of their wrongdoings like that. They probably have moved on and are enjoying life while you are still stuck in the yesteryear. Remember, no storm lasts forever. Sunshine is on the other side of the clouds.

Step 9 It Is What It Is

The world is what it is, and people are who they are. Quit trying to analyze every minute situation and people's behaviors. When you remove something out of your life you create a void. That void needs to be filled up so that there are no existing gaps in your life. What it means is, when you forgive and let go, you have removed the anger, hurts, resentment, and pain. Then, what is left is a gap. Fill that gap with love and see that life will flow smoothly. Love conquers all obstacles in life. As humans, we will always meet people that want to push our buttons. These people are shallow minded so do not stoop to their level. They need redemption, pray for them. Fighting people like this is not worth it.

8

FINDING STRENGTH

salm 68:5 says, *"God is the father of the fatherless and a husband to the widow."*

So, God will always fight your battles for you, you just need to trust him.

Once you have given forgiveness and received forgiveness, there is a need to stay in that forgiveness mode. Here are tips to help you remain positive.

20 Tips on Staying Strong

1. Sometimes it's better never to show your weaknesses to people as they will take advantage of your weakness. This is common in some families. When you are widowed, the very people who are supposed to help you and support you may be the biggest cause of your pain and struggles.
2. Accept the grieving process. Taking shortcuts in the grieving and the healing process will always have terrible repercussions. Learn to laugh the pain away, as bottling it up will cause you to erupt at any given chance.
3. Take care of your physical and mental health that way you will be stable enough to make your own decisions. Your body is your passport to a happy and healthy life.
4. Hang around like-minded people who have a good vision for their

future.

5. Remember no one knows you and your children more than you do. Take control of your life. Don't wait for people to lead you astray.

6. Live in the present. Don't drive your car looking in the rear-view mirror. There is a reason that it was made smaller than the windshield.

7. What does not kill you makes you stronger. So, if you are not dead because of the struggles and frustrations of widowhood and divorce, then move on.

8. Be kind to others as Karma will not forget the address of those that hurt you. Being kind has some ripple effects. What you put out there will find its way back to you.

9. Don't look down upon yourself because you are a widow, a single mom, and that you cannot fight for your dreams. If you don't fight for your dreams, then someone will pay you to build those dreams for them.

10. Choose your friends wisely. Choose those that will help you grow, not those that will continue to pull you down and suck the life out of you. When you meet people like that, run away as far away from them as you can.

11. Trust your gut or intuition all the time. As women, we have this gift of intuition, use and grow it.

12. Revenge is sweet, but forgiveness is sweeter.

13. Meet new people every time. It broadens your horizon so that you are not narrow-minded. It's not written anywhere that widows and divorcees cannot meet people and learn new things. I beg to be corrected.

14. Use the success of other people, widowed or not, single mothers or in nuclear families to inspire yourself. Don't wallow in your grief.

15. Go into the world expecting to be rejected. That way when it happens it does not hit you hard and throw you overboard. Go ahead and ask for some impossible things from people. You will be surprised how many people will help you, simply because you asked them.

16. Don't hide your ignorance. Take that as a learning tool and use it to your advantage. Use your failures as a stepping stone to greater heights.

17. Stop being a perfectionist. No one is perfect. Learn from those imperfections and let them be a lesson in life.

18. Do not rely on other people's opinions of your life. Make your own decisions as people will tell you what works for them, not for you. Do what works for you.

19. Refuse to be defined by your widow status. Surprise people with your achievements and never rely solely on other people to help you out all the time.

20. Allow yourself to be a normal person who accepts their flaws. No one is perfect in the world.

Forgiveness has taught me to be the better person. I have forgiven my in-laws for what they did to me when my husband died. Now I feel so much better and we are in good talking terms. We visit each other, talk and laugh on the phone. I discovered that holding onto the pain and resentment was not going to change what happened. I might not forget it, but it does not make it okay that they hurt me like that. What happened then was painful and shameful. I hope they learned from it because I did. I learned that you cannot rely on people's opinions of you to be happy. What people say about you will not change who you are inside. It might alter your thinking and behavior, but inside you are still the same person.

Nothing can upset you and derail your thoughts unless you give it consent and power to control you.

The pain I went through is the reason I decided to write this book so that other people can learn from it. It's normal for people to hurt you, but it is what you do with the hurts, wounds, frustrations, hate, anger and the shame that matters. Don't waste your pain, use it for your own good, learn from it, and move on.

What does not kill you, makes you stronger. It's called life, live it, dwelling on the past will not make it go away. So, look at it and move on.

9

EXIT THE DARK PLACE INTO TRANSFORMATION

B eing a widow takes a toll on your life, emotionally, mentally, physically and psychologically. The other party that will feed off this negative energy is your children. Sometimes as a widow, you can get swallowed up in trying to fix everything else out there that you forget those closest to you, which is yourself and, your children. I am talking from experience having walked that road too. The pain is huge. When you have been used to raising the children with your spouse and sharing the running of the home financially, it becomes overwhelming for your small brain.

But when you put your mind to it, nothing is impossible.

You can do this!!

To make lasting and significant changes in your life, in order to make a fresh start, you must take the bull by the horns. Get out of your comfort zone so you can create this new beginning. The children will look up to you for support and you are their pillar and sometimes you will be all that is left for them. This might be because there are no ties with the in-laws or your own family. After you have gone through the healing process it is important to make sure that you do not fall off the wagon after all the hard work. You must create an environment that is not conducive to going back to your ***Pity Party self***. You need to remind yourself how important it is to stay afloat and forge ahead so that the healing process is never a wasted process.

The transformation includes changing your thought process and how you visualize the world moving ahead. It will also include your actions towards life; how you interact with yourself as well as others. It involves keeping in touch with your support system so that you do not fall through the cracks. Transformation is a healing process. It's continuous and is not achieved overnight. Use the little strength left in your body to keep your head above all the issues otherwise those issues will drown you. You should be thankful that at least you have survived this far, to be able to read this book so it can help you to put the pieces together. You have managed to look after the children and helped them through their mourning and grieving processes. Remember you are not alone; help is out there you just need to ask for it. Now is the time to look after YOU so you can be able to continue looking after the children.

If you do not go through the transformational process you will continue to survive, but never live and thrive again. You did a good thing and you created a life with your late husband, now you need to let go and work on you. This might sound selfish but, I'm sure that when you look back, you'll see my point that it is time to focus on changing things around a bit. The transformation will help you not to remain stuck, looking at the world through a tinted glass.

Remember you are the captain of your own ship, and you have the power to change your life and live the life you deserve, happy.

This process of transformation is going to build you from the old weak and vulnerable you to the more focused and happier going you. Remember life still moves forward with or without you. What you have gone through as a widow should make you strong. Take that experience as a building block for your new life.

Difficult Decisions in The Transformation Process

Sometimes you must make some tough decisions in order to make significant changes in your life. I packed my bags and left for North America. I cried all the way on my two-day journey, but I had done it. I spoke to my children about my plans to leave the country. Although it was hard to predict what was going to happen to us, we agreed that I had to leave. My family was in support of this considering what was going on in my life at that time. I saw that living the life I was living, was not going to pay any dividends to my children.

When I got to North America, I went through culture shock, food shock, people shock, language shock, dressing shock, driving shock. It was so different from what I was used to. People drove on the wrong side of the road. The English language was spoken differently here. They did not speak the queen's language which I had grown up listening to and speaking. So, you can imagine what went through my head.

When I left my mother country Zimbabwe, I thought things were going to be different, but not so vast a difference. I could not find a job for a while. I was a College lecturer when I left my motherland. I never knew that my qualifications would not meet up to the American standard. So, I could not work as a lecturer anymore. I started working in Assisted Living places as a Personal Care Assistant. This was hard for me, but I had to do it in order to feed the three children, and of course myself.

I am so thankful to my friend Kezina and her husband, Willard, who took care of me when I arrived in America. They helped me with the application process for the American visa. I left America after three years and moved to Canada. I could not make it in the States for some reason. Everything kept hitting a brick wall and I had to make another bold move. I arrived in Canada in 2006 and it took me some time to get all the paperwork organized so I could start working. I had the same issue; finding work. Instead of sitting and crying about it, I decided I would go back to school. With the minimum wage, I was getting from my three jobs, I sponsored myself through university again. I did Social Work and another degree in Sociology through

Athabasca University.

It was easier to do the degree online so I could continue working. It was now about 6 years since I had seen my children. Every day was getting harder to stay without them. I had started the immigration process and it required lots of money. Being an immigrant is not fun, especially when you are separated from your children and there is no husband to look after them. I was lucky my family helped me a lot. I also want to thank the boarding schools that they were at. They knew my situation and did the best they could to keep my children safe and comfortable.

After getting my Diploma in Social Work, I got a better job as a Program Coordinator. That was such a relief. Then, I had more money to start preparing the paperwork for my children's visas and also complete my Bachelor's Degree in Sociology. Recently, I put myself through some self-development school. I am a certified International Transformation Coach. I am also an internationally certified relationship and dating expert. I decided to write this book, to help transform the lives of so many widows. To top it off, I am also a certified Reiki Master and Angelic Healer.

The day when my children's visas were approved was the best day of my life. It had been six years since I had seen my children. It was on October 21st, 2008 when I finally got an email from Canadian Immigration Visa office in Pretoria, South Africa, that my children's visas had been issued. I was ecstatic. I was screaming, rolling on the floor, jumping up and down, crying and thanking God at the same time. Three weeks later, I was at the airport waiting for them.

As I was waiting for the arrivals, I heard my name being called through the intercom. I thought, "Oh my, now what?" Apparently, I had to sign for my youngest daughter as she was still a minor. Still, I had not seen them. It was only after I signed the paperwork, did the immigration officer open the sliding glass door and I saw my three children. I screamed, they screamed, and it was chaos. Security guards came running. They thought someone had been attacked. Only to see an emotional family reunion. It was so emotional. I will never forget that feeling and that moment. I still have that first picture with them at the airport and treasure this picture.

Sometimes in order to make that shift in your life, be prepared to take some risks. It worked for me. I can only imagine if I had stayed and continued to live that, "poor me" life. What would have become of me? And worse, my children?

Ask yourself. What bold decisions do you have to make in order to get that transformation in your life right now?

24 Tips for Transformation

Take care of your health, body, and soul (more in the next chapter under self-care). Without a healthy you, then there is no transformation possible.

1. Remember, losing your spouse does not change your soul/spirit. You are still the same individual with some bumps and bruises, but your soul is still the same. No one touches your soul except you, and God, your creator. Remember God created you in his image. You are precious.

2. Be kind to yourself and everyone around you. When you treat other people with respect you are letting love into your life and others. Allow yourself to ask for help if you need it, let people help you, no one can survive in a vacuum. You will need people around to give you moral support and cheer you on.

3. Be a good listener, do not be quick to react, and never enjoy having the last word in every conflict or conversation.

4. Do not hold onto your past hurts. Let them go and allow things to happen in your life. Let bygones be bygones. Forgive others in the process and see how other people will forgive you too.

5. Listen to your intuition or your gut feeling. It always gives you the best alert when things are not right.

6. Respect other people's time and don't think that because you are a widow you should get special treatment. If people offer it, then accept. However, do not demand it like it's your right. Don't give yourself a sense of entitlement to other people's life. That is being selfish.

7. Learn to forgive yourself if you have let yourself down. Let it go. I know

you might say it's easier said than done. Yet, what good does it bring you, holding onto the bitter past or beating yourself up? When you forgive yourself, you are freeing yourself from the bondage of misery.

8. Learn to be present in each moment so that you do not lose focus on what you are doing to achieve your goals, as tomorrow is never promised. This could be going back to work, going through the widowhood tasks and so on.

9. Learn meditation and mindfulness, as they help to slow down your mind and rejuvenate your energy.

10. Do not aim to be perfect in everything but do the best you can. This reduces your anxiety and stress levels enormously.

11. You cannot control everyone and how they will treat you but remember you can control how you will respond or react to their behavior. Nothing can upset you unless you give it consent to do so.

12. Never stop learning new things. This will keep you abreast of the ever-changing world and life skills. Learn how to use technology. This can be challenging if you are over 45 years and trying to learn this for the first time. Have your kids assist you. I struggle with gadgets, but my kids are my safety net. Learning new things keeps your brain young and that will affect your interaction with the world.

13. Don't always focus on your problems but look at the problems as a learning challenge to find solutions. Be solution-focused. No more pity parties, but victory parties for all your successes.

14. Check your belief systems and see if they still work for you or against you. Sometimes our own belief systems keep us in bondage. This can also be affected by how you grew up. Most of the time we practice what has been exposed to us by our parents especially our mothers. Ask yourself, what are your children learning from your experience?

15. Look at your values, what is important to you? How does that shape who you are? Your values build who you are and give you the foundation to rebuild your life.

16. Spend time with good people that will teach you something new, that will help you to grow. This is also the time to review your friends.

Sometimes keeping too many people around that do not help you to grow will weigh you down and keep you stuck in your misery. Ditch the energy drainers because they are not worth your time anymore.

17. Do things that make you happy.
18. Do not waste time judging others and their faults or you will also be judged. Use that time and energy to grow yourself.
19. Do not give in to fear, as fear has no idea how much strength you have. You are reading this book now because you have decided to ditch the "poor me" life and take the high road to a new and prosperous life.
20. Learn to say NO to things that you are not comfortable doing. This will stop people from taking advantage of you, and your vulnerability as a widow or divorcee.
21. Don't put your life on autopilot. Learn to change things around you regularly, like the clothes you wear, your daily routine, the foods that you eat and even the places you go to do your shopping.
22. Make sure you balance your life, between work, family and time for yourself.
23. Never make conditions for your happiness. Like waiting to be happy until you've solved all the widowhood tasks. If you are happy now, it will give you more energy to work through the tasks faster and more efficiently than when you are dragging yourself around.
24. Remember to take every new day as a blessing to you and know that healing is behind your fear.

Transformation is like removing makeup at the end of the day and looking at your face and still seeing yourself as beautiful as ever!!

10

GRATEFUL PEOPLE WIN

"Gratitude is more of a compliment to yourself than someone else." R Farooq

Gratitude is a selfless act that is done unconditionally to show people that they are appreciated. It's free and with no effort required to give it.

Let's imagine you are having the worst day of your life and someone just comes, gives you a big hug and tells you that everything is going to be alright. They even tell you that you are a very strong woman and you will pull through. What would you say to this stranger? A thank you, would be appropriate. How do you think that person feels after you give them gratitude for giving you that hug?

Another example is all those people that stood by you during and after the funeral. Some of them gave a lot of their time just to be with you and never asked for anything in return. Remember that person that you never expected to show up at the funeral and they walked in, gave you a huge hug and wiped your tears from your face? Remember the feeling you had? You were grateful that they came right? That's gratitude. I'm sure you said thank you to them too.

Gratitude can be very contagious. It's like smiling. It makes the world a happier place to live in. Just being grateful every day makes you a happier person. Stop being critical about everything in life. Since you are now a widow, ask yourself what are you grateful for? Do not tell me that there is nothing left in your present life that you are grateful for?

For example, you are alive today and reading this book, that's something you should be grateful for. If you have a roof over your head, that's another thing too. Do you drive a car? Do you have children? Do you have good health? Do you have money to put some food on the table? It might not be that much, but with time things will change? You still have eyes to see, ears to hear, legs and feet to walk with, a back to stand upon and some hair on your head.

Another reason to be grateful is, someone was in love with you so much that they took to the altar you both said I DO, and you were someone's wife for a while. That's why you are now a widow. Someone was bold enough to forsake all other women for you!

There is a lot for us to be grateful for. As humans we have a list of things that we feel should be done for us to be grateful. Yes, you should be grateful because both you and your spouse could be no more. Meaning that your children could be orphans. If you are still facing challenges in this widowhood journey, then be grateful that this book is available for you to learn from.

Be grateful because you are alive today as tomorrow is never promised to anyone.

Benefits of Expressing Gratitude

- Being a grateful human being is said to improve our overall health and well-being. Being an ungrateful and bitter person increases stress, high blood pressure, and anxiety levels.
- A grateful person creates and strengthens interpersonal relationships, and this creates an environment of forgiveness for each other.
- Happy people are those that express their gratitude to others. This will, in turn, make people show their gratitude to you as well.
- Showing gratitude helps you to create more friendships. You just create this welcoming energy that attracts people or invites people to your circle.

- Gratitude creates less self-centeredness in people, which will, as a result, create more optimism. Gratitude also creates higher levels of self-esteem; more self-confidence and the result is a happier world.

- Gratitude creates happier moods that will improve your sleep, increase your energy as well as keep you healthier unlike if you are being an ungrateful and grouchy person. You will drain more energy by being a negative person. Grateful people fall asleep faster than ungrateful ones because they are not struggling with anything in their minds. You will not waste time on things you have no control over. If you have a lot of things that are worrying you, then you will not sleep well right? You can call gratitude a sleep aid and by the way, it's free!

- Gratitude will also improve your decision-making process, as you will be more focused on a healthy brain.

- Gratitude makes you recognize the benevolence around you which will, in turn, make people kinder to you and you to them. You will be able to receive help from people and you will be able to offer your help to other people too. I wish the world was full of more grateful people. I understand that you cannot make people be grateful when they are not. Your task on this earth is about you and the world that you are trying to create. People will always emulate good things especially your children. Do not let the loss of your spouse turn you into an ungrateful widow who is so hard to get along with.

- Gratitude helps us to cope with pain. You are grateful and then you can think beyond your limiting beliefs that insist that you will never be happy again. If you are a grateful person, it helps to bounce back from your rock bottom **Widow's** life.

- Gratitude will help you to be thankful for the life you lived with your spouse and the memories that you created together. Those memories will give you the strength to withstand any frustrations that might come your way. Those happy memories will make you smile even on your worst days.

- Gratitude makes you less envious of other people's achievements and lives. Instead, it will give you a boost to improve your life.

- Gratitude is a relaxant that comes free to humankind. Imagine that you are just being happy every day. You stop worrying about a lot of things, you are also less stressed out about things, life would be great.
- Gratitude makes you a better parent, as you will not be so critical of your children and their way of grieving.
- Keep a gratitude journal to help you keep track of the things to be thankful for and make sure it's updated regularly or daily in the morning before you start your day. That way the list will remind you of how lucky you are to have what you have. It could have been worse.
- Don't keep gratitude to yourself, please share it, so that it creates positive ripple effects of love and peace.

How to experience gratitude daily in your life

- **Spend Time with People That Mean A Lot to You.** This is a great way for you to show your gratitude to them for being there for you. There could be some family members that are just difficult to deal with no matter how nice you are to them. My advice is to stop fighting with them just show them lots of gratitude. I tell you, it works. They will not understand what hit them to get that much gratitude from a person that they expected fire from. Just be nice to them and love will conquer all. Sometimes fighting with people and trying to change them takes a lot of energy. Just letting people be who they are is much easier.
- **Stop Being A Perfectionist.** Accepting people as they are and things, as they are, is a great way to start. No one is perfect in the world and neither are you perfect too.
- **Take Time to Smell the Fresh Morning Breeze.** Thank God for another day added to your calendar. You could have died in your sleep, but here you are enjoying another day in your life.
- **Take Your Challenges as A Stepping Stone.** Most challenges keep your brain sharp as you think to find solutions. Without them, you forget to think or be active in your creativity.
- **Always Be Grateful for What You Have and Who You Are.** You are

unique and special to you. Keep a gratitude journal that you write your daily gratitude list. Keep track of your positive thoughts, and don't waste time on negative thoughts as they will not solve your issues. The gratitude journal helps you to see what you should be grateful for in your life.

• **Share Gratitude with Others.** Share your gratitude with others and see how it comes back to you.

A lot of us express gratitude when we have everything going for us. Gratitude, in all honesty, is authentic when we accept support and challenges, triumphs and defeats, opportunity and obstacles, pleasures and pain. Life is not a one size fits all garment.

Be thankful even in widowhood for your spouse who left you some treasured memories. You had a husband; some people have not even gotten married their whole lifetime. This might sound harsh, but I am speaking to the widow reading this book. I was bitter for the longest while as I could not understand how I could get widowed at such a young age. I was in my thirties and had been together with my husband for only 13 years before he passed away. To me, that was a slap in the face. I came to realize that everyone has their own destiny and you cannot compare your life to that of others, as we all have different life spans. But it just hurts I know.

Now ask yourself:

What did I learn from this **Widowhood** journey?

How has it changed my life into the person I am today?

How can I help someone else who is going through what I went through as a widow/divorcee?

When you look at your life today what are you most grateful for?

Being negative in that widow mode has not helped any widow I know. So, quit it and let's get you back on track again. I have realized that life will go on with or without you.

Always talk from a place of love, not hurt, anger, judgment or criticism. These nasty things always create resentment in a person. Talking from a place of love will help keep all the negativity from your space and thus attracting the universe to help you achieve the healing of your wounds, pains, and fears.

Help Through Visualization and Imagination

Visualization is a process of forming mental visual images. It's using your imagination to create an image of the future you are hoping to achieve. Your job now will be to bring those visual images to reality by working towards those visualizations.

The process works like this:

See It

Close your eyes and create an image of things you are longing for. The big changes in your life. This could be things like, getting your kids through college, getting a new job, a new house, a new car, even getting healthy if you are not feeling well, or maybe meeting another man who is going to be your husband.

Feel It

Let your mind start feeling it as if it has already happened in your life. Let your emotions be drawn to feeling this energy too. Your emotions will connect with your subconscious mind and that picture will stick in your brain. It's like a camera taking pictures and storing them in your subconscious mind. Remember the joy you had when you achieved your goal?

Putting this image and that joy in the past will remove the feeling of fear of not getting what you wanted. It removes that void that you might feel when you have not gotten what you wanted. When you feel it, it becomes reality to you it's no longer in the "**what if**" zone. Now focus on the abundance and not lack. So, everything you desire to happen in your future, see it now and feel it in your bones. This way you have a positive vibe around you attracting positive energy which will, in turn, let the Law of Attraction start to work for you. If you cannot feel it, then look for what is blocking you to get this feeling and work towards diminishing those blockages.

Be it

Once you start feeling it, then let it manifest and then you become it. Now you are living as if you have already enjoyed your goal, your vision or your visualization. It's now in the Manifestation Stage as it has come true. Once you believe that you are it, you will see things starting to point you in that direction. Use lots of positive Affirmations to keep you in that mindset and never allow any doubts or negative thinking to bring you off course.

So, visualization activates the power of your brain to make your goals or mental images into reality. In visualization, there is what is called the "**Law of Returns**." It's like Karma. What you send out is what you will get. So, when you visualize, make sure it's positive visualization. If you visualize negative thoughts for someone, it will be sent back to you. Remember Karma does not forget your address.

Visualization and manifestation work hand in hand. When you visualize what you want in your mind, write it down so that it's engraved in your mind and this will help the manifestation process as the subconscious mind is already activated. Your mind power will then make it look real as you will start to see it happening before it manifests. That's helpful to keep you in a positive space of mind. Manifestations can be delayed if you have self-doubts in your process. Be positive and the Law of Attraction will work for you.

6 Benefits of Visualization

Health Benefits

I mentioned at the beginning of this chapter that your mind creates your life for you. So, what you visualize is what you will manifest. Studies have shown that what happens in the mind can also create diseases in your body. High blood pressure, anxiety, and ulcers are mostly caused by letting the negative thoughts to turn into reality. You get very stressed out and send your body into sicknesses. Imagine the way you feel when you think that something bad is going to happen to you, or if you are driving in the snow and you picture yourself in a rollover accident. My God, that makes your stomach turn right? If the negative thoughts have that impact on you then imagine having positive thoughts and visualizations?

Refocusing

Life as a widow can be overwhelming at times. Your thoughts can get muddled up as a lot is going on at the same time. Visualization can help you to refocus on your goals and help to get back on track. One way to do this is to take 5 to 10 minutes of your time before going to sleep and just lie on your bed face up.

- Close your eyes for a moment in a quiet space.
- Just let your body loose and listen to your breathing or put on some soft relaxing music. Just let all the tension in your body go and feel relaxed.
- Start to imagine the life you want to build for yourself.
- Allow yourself to go into that life and consume that positive energy. While you are there, you will feel your emotions starting to change as they embrace that positive energy.
- Release all the negative images, letting go of all the "**what ifs**" and replacing them with the positive images. Tell yourself that "I deserve to be happy and start a new life." This will activate the mind power to support your image, helping your visualization to manifest and come to reality.

Bear in mind you can also visualize as go about your day. Just take some quiet time and relax, then start visualizing. Take that image and let it guide your activities for the day.

Optimize Performance

This visualization technique is also used by many athletes to improve their performance. They are told to visualize winning the game or race and they will go on the arena all hyped up to defeat the other team. Remember that you are the boss of your thoughts. Your thoughts come from your brain, so you can control them. If you cannot do it, then find out why. As soon as you create space in your mind for success, the brain will start to process ways to meet those goals to manifest it and it will shift your life in a positive direction.

As a widow, you need to start visualizing your future self all healed up and starting another chapter of your life. Always remind yourself that life does not come with a manual, you have to write your own as you go.

Increase Positive Thoughts

Visualization will help you to stay positive. This happens when you have positive self-talk which will create positive visualizations. So be mindful of the thoughts you have during the day as you go on with your daily activities. Always visualize your life with a good ending. One thing to remember is this will not happen overnight. It takes time to manifest so you must give it time to come to pass. It's a continuous repetition of the positive thoughts that will shift things over time.

Increase Motivation

Remember I spoke about seeing things or your achieved goals or life in the past. This means that you imagine yourself having achieved the goals already and having that mindset will uplift your mood, and increase your motivation. You are going to be in a good and celebratory mood as you are excited about your achievement. You will always be a happy person and overtime it will help you to feel better and happier. Soon the poor me mindset will vanish.

Diminish Negativity

As you visualize positive thoughts it creates a positive environment around you which will, in turn, diminish all the negativity around you. Focus more on what you want to achieve in life and your children. This helped me to stay focused as I would remind myself about the goals I had set for the kids and myself. I wanted to stay away from all the misery that the death of my husband had brought into my life. So, after realizing that pity parties did not change anything in my life, I refocused my attention on defining what I wanted my life to be. It worked for me and today I have written this book to help other women see that there is life after a gloomy period as a widow.

The Benefits of Visualization in Summary;

- It activates your subconscious to find creative ideas to achieve your goals.
- It activates your brain to find the resources you will need to achieve your new life.
- It creates a positive environment that will activate the Law of Attraction. As a result, good people will come into your life to help you achieve your goals.
- It increases your motivation levels, thereby reducing stress and any other health issues that come as a result of the stressful widowhood journey you are walking in.
- Remember your mind goes where your energy is. So, be careful what you spend your time doing.

Reframing your Negative Thoughts

Reframing your mind is like retraining your brain. As hard as it might sound, you still must focus on your "why." Remind yourself why dwelling on the negative thoughts will not change your situation, but just make it worse. Sometimes not focusing on your "why" will make you comfortable and your mind will get muddled up again.

As a widow, you might be living with the mindset that you are supposed to be sad. You might think it is to show the in-laws, your family, friends and the rest of the world that you are really grieving the death of your husband. I did that, and I tell you it does not work at all. Yes, you can grieve and mourn the loss of your husband but being happy is a personal choice. Of course, you cannot be seen laughing everywhere you go, like you swallowed laughing gas!

Being sad all the time and being surrounded by negative thoughts has severe effects on your health and those around you. During the grieving process, there should be some days when you feel down, but you must be able to find things that can cheer you up so you can be in a positive mood.

The first few days after the funeral, you might not feel like talking or even smiling. That's ok. As time goes on, you need to slowly be able to come out of your shell and join the normal world. Being sad is not going to bring your husband back. This might sound harsh or selfish. If you live your life according to the approval of others, you will be stuck in the "pity party" or "poor me" world, forever. Do not be a people pleaser, because you will never please everyone, including yourself. So, quit being sad months or years after your husband is gone. That will not solve any of the issues you will be facing. I got to a point where I had lost weight and all my clothes were falling off me. I had lost my joy. This was because I had surrounded myself with all these negative people that kept telling me that having fun or being fun on the street was not being respectful to my late husband. I had seen widows in my local town behaving like that, so I believed it for a while. Those that seemed to be outgoing were labeled as "uncouth widows." I did not want to disgrace my parents since they lived in the same city as me.

My dad had a conversation with me 18 months after the funeral. He asked me how long I was going to be holding those pity parties? He reminded me that even if I continued to live that, "poor me" life it was not going to help me pay the bills, send my kids to school, or bring Temba back. I know there was a lot that was happening in my life after losing my husband. I thought to myself about what my dad had said, and it dawned on me that he was right. My health had deteriorated a lot because I was not sleeping well and not eating well either. My children also were of the same opinion as my dad. I looked into my children's eyes and I thought to myself I still had a reason to live and be there for my children. That day was my turning point. My best friend, Cecilia, had had that conversation with me, but I did not take her seriously. Her situation was way different from mine as she had been divorced for a while. She was free to do whatever she wanted. For me, because I was still carrying my married name, I felt it was a different ball game. The question **what will people say?** had been echoing in my ears for the longest while and it had held me hostage.

Now I have learned that letting other people control your life is the worst thing that you can ever do to yourself. These other people have their lives to live and you have your own. While they whisper behind your back, when they see you in a joyful mood, they will still talk behind your back if you have lost your groove. People will still talk no matter what. You can never meet up to anybody's standards. Not everyone is going to like you, and not everyone is going to be your friend either.

Finally, I realized that the sad or negative mindset had not changed my situation one bit. I thought to myself that I had gone through hell since the death of my husband. So, what else was going to pull me down, that I had not experienced already? A choice to make changes to how I was going to live the rest of my life had to be made. I used to be a happy go person with a very bubbly personality but all that had since been lost with the grieving. All my glow and beautiful smile had vanished. Why was I doing this to myself? The grieving period had to come to an end so I could start focusing on my new life.

Here are Some Examples of Negative Thoughts

"I am so done with trying."
   "It's so hard to focus."
   "I will never get over this pain."
   "My life will never be the same again since becoming a widow."
   "Is there anything wrong with me?"
   "Life is not fair, why me?"
   "I will never be normal again."
   "I will never find another love of my life."
   "I should have never married him in the first place."
   "Why did this happen to me?"

The Revised Version as Positive Thoughts

"Giving up is not an option."

"I will keep trying. I know I can do this."

"I am starting my healing journey now and I will find help."

"My life will change even though I am a widow."

"Life is what I will make it."

"I will find someone else to love and to love me."

"I married him because I loved him."

Stop asking **why** it happened to you. Start asking **what** you can do to change your situation.

The Reframing Processes.

- The first step for me was to have the **awareness** that something had to change in my life. I realized that the negative thoughts I had entertained had not given me any peace of mind. I had suffered sleepless nights, poor appetite, loss of some friends, and was very lonely. This was now affecting my children as I had lost my old self that was always happy and in a joyous mood.

- The second step was to ask me some **sincere questions.** "Why was I letting myself feel so unhappy? What was I getting out of all the sadness? How could I change my life? How did I let myself be in that situation?"

- The third step is to start the **reframing process**. This is not as easy as it sounds. I am not trying to discourage you, but I am just being honest. It is like the healing process. You must want to reframe your mind, and no one can do this for you. The process of reframing looks at the now and the future, not the past. How are you going to be living your life? How are you going to control your mindset, what about your thinking process from now moving forward? You must scan your own mind to see which areas you need to control. Once you know which areas have been dragging you down you deal with those areas in the present. Once you realize that you have control over your thoughts, you will be able to move out of that negative mindset. One thing that I realized, was that the negative thoughts and negative people will always be there, but I had to control how they affected me. I also had a choice over entertaining the negative or positive thoughts and negative people. So, if I felt sad then it meant that I had made the choice to let that negativity affect me. This process was hard to comprehend, but I had to do it, and so can you. You just need to be patient with yourself.

2 Types of Negative Thoughts

1. **Unproductive Negative** thoughts that serve you no purpose. These are very common as they feel comfortable for most widows. They make you feel as if you still belong with your husband. You feel that you don't have to do anything positive to change your situation. Being sad is the norm.

2. **Negative thoughts** that are action-oriented. These come, like your gut feeling telling you something is not right and needs you to act. This could be some behaviors or moods that need to be changed in order to make life easy for people around you. Sometimes it happens when you transfer your anger onto other innocent people that had nothing to do with whatever made you angry. I'm sure you have seen people that just lash out at you for no reason at all.

How to Reframe the Unproductive Negative Thoughts

1. **Ignore them**

These are thoughts that tell you, "You should not have married that guy in the first place, now you are a widow. You should have done more to save the life of your husband, or you did not grieve long enough you should be ashamed of yourself." These are the thoughts that you should tell to "buzz off". They are not doing any good. They only make you feel guilty, sending you into a regret mode.

1. **Change Your Focus**

Asking yourself truthful questions usually helps, as it will jolt your mind to rethink and refocus. The other way is to keep your mind busy doing some new stuff to divert your attention. Playing games with your kids or keeping busy with things that require you to think. The other way would be to label that thought as unproductive and you will see yourself refocusing. Try to reshape the problem and that way you will see it with a different perspective. Just practice it over and over.

How to Stop Dwelling on the Negative Thoughts

Reframe Your Situation

If you are late for an appointment for one of the widowhood tasks, call them and advise them you are running late, instead of crying and complaining about it. If you get caught up in traffic, take this as a time to reflect on your day and plan for the following day. Always carry a book to read, or do word searches or crossword puzzles, if you are on a bus, train, or plane. Learn new things.

Stop for A Drink or Cup of Tea

If you a feeling lonely and isolated, go out for a drink or hot chocolate or tea. A cup of tea will soothe you and make you feel better and more relaxed. If you cannot sleep at night have a glass of warm milk and get a hot water bottle in your bed that will keep you warm and comfortable.

Take A Warm Shower or Bath

Taking a long warm shower or bath will get you very relaxed and that can release all the tension in your body and mind. Sing your favorite songs while you are at it. It helps to redirect your thoughts.

Throw the Negative Thoughts Away

Take a piece of paper, write the negative thoughts that are bugging you. Tear that piece of paper and throw it away. It helps to purge all the negative thoughts from your mind onto a piece of paper and into the trash can.

Start A Morning Positive Ritual

Take 5 to 10 minutes in the morning to meditate. If you cannot meditate, pray for a few minutes, go through your to-do list. Tell yourself that it's going to be a positive day and you are ready for it. If you fear something, ask yourself how you can deal with that issue beforehand. That way you are not anxious as you go into the day. Have a positive mindset as you start your day.

Don't Be A Perfectionist

Trying to be perfect and expecting everyone to be perfect is too much to ask from yourself and the world. Give yourself and the world the benefit of the doubt. If you fail, let it be a learning curve for you. Remember people are different and behave differently too. You have no control over how people think and behave, but you have control over what you think and how you feel.

Replacement Theory

Whenever you get a negative thought creeping into your mind, acknowledge it. Don't dwell on it before replacing that thought with a positive thought. This can be hard at first, but once you get the hang of it, you can even laugh at the negative thoughts and give it a name. That way if it comes back again you can call it by name and tell it to zoom off! Ask that negative problem why it keeps coming back, sometimes you can get an idea of why it keeps coming back.

Look for Triggers

If the negative thoughts keep coming back over and over, then look for triggers. Is it the environment, or the company of the people you are with that keep reminding you of certain things? It could be a smell, colors, food, etc. Check it out and see if anything could be a trigger. Be vigilant, because practice makes perfect.

In conclusion, reframing your mind to stop dwelling on negative thoughts can be challenging at first. As time goes, it becomes easier. You just must keep practising and being vigilant about it. Always remember your "why." Bear in mind you have control over your thoughts and how you let them affect you.

"You cannot think negative and have a positive life. Meaning you cannot sow tomato seeds and expect pepper fruits."
— **Oscar Bimpong**

So, think twice before dwelling on a negative thought.

Scared to be an emotionally unavailable mom

I decided to work on reframing the negative thoughts and focused on my healing so I can be there for my children. I had heard about families that were being torn apart because of the surviving parent consumed by their grief, and forgetting about their children. I learned that when parents become emotionally unavailable, that causes children to have some serious behavioural issues.

Children can start to be attention seekers in various ways just to get that parental love they miss from home. I wanted to be there physically and emotionally for my children. They had lost one parent already and I did not want them to lose me as well when I could do something about it. I soon discovered that children who were raised in an unemotionally available environment would suffer from trust issues, attachment issues, and an inability to maintain a connection with other people. Some children can end up getting some quick fix to this void in their lives like drugs or seek attention in the wrong places. Children raised from emotionally neglected homes have a tendency of developing self-doubt and this grows with them into their adulthood. This scared me. That my children would end up attracting some emotionally unavailable romantic partners or friends. I did not want them to look for love elsewhere when I was still alive to give it to them.

So, think about it for a while, when you want to continue entertaining negative thoughts. Cut them off it's not worth it.

Before I left for North America, we prayed in our little circle just the four of us. My kids said to me, "Mama no matter what people are saying and will say, we know you love us, and we trust you, and one day we will be reunited."

This is the promise that I kept to my kids, I will never forget this. Whatever I did, was to make sure that I remain focused on that promise. Sometimes you need these kinds of goals and promises to keep you focused.

The day we were reunited is the day I will never forget. I kept on telling myself, *"I kept my promise and I did it."*

Lord thank you!

Thank you, God!

I could almost not believe it as I looked into the same eyes of my children six years later.

11

FINDING YOUR IDENTITY AFTER GRIEF OR LOSS

When you lose a spouse, your identity is altered greatly, to suit those changes in your life at that time. You are perceived differently by the same people that knew you before that traumatic event took place. It's funny that this only affects women. For men they don't change their last names, the only thing they will do is change their status and take off their rings. For women, it's emotionally draining and it will cost money to go back to your maiden name. Maybe, that's why some women nowadays prefer to use their maiden names even after they marry. So, from a Mrs., you now must go back to a Miss again or Ms., while the men will remain Mr., whether married, single, divorced or widowed, it's unfair for the women though.

Whenever I was completing forms, writing my marital status, was a struggle at first. I had to stop for a while and remember that I was still married to my husband, but I cannot put that on paper anymore because he is no longer here. I had to cross out married and put widowed with tears running down my cheeks. This took me a while to get used to it. The marriage certificate is still with me to this day, but it's no longer valid anymore. I keep it in case I need to prove that I was married to my late husband for some reason or another. This is the worst part.

As you become a widow you become adapted to many identities.

Rational Identity

This identity changes when a situation changes. If you took care of your husband during his ill health, then you became his caregiver. At the same time, you were still his wife and the mother of his children. So now that he is gone, you are no longer his caregiver, you become his widow overnight. That is very hard to adjust to overnight. During this process you lose your sanity due to grief and some people might say things like, "she is nuts, she has lost it." How soon people forget about the overnight switch of roles and identities you just went through. People look at you differently as your identity has changed. In your family, for example, you are no longer identified as the same person. To your in-laws, you are the daughter in law of their late son. When you visit them, you don't feel like you belong there anymore. There is that feeling you get like your season has just passed and they seem to be waiting to see what your next plans are. This also creates another shift in your rational identity. There is that distance between you and them. Sometimes they can still treat you with the same respect as before, but this also depends on the different cultures and beliefs. Has anything like this happened to you?

You might have to move houses and so your address changes. You must make new friends and start to introduce yourself all over again as who now? "Oh, I was married, but now I am a widow." Even if you do not mention it, your status will come up in one way or another. As time goes on, they would want to know about your status or your family. "Oh, you have kids, and how is their dad doing?" There comes the painful part. Now I must repeat my story again. You lose who you are in this process. People around you do not realize that you are battling to gain some identity that keeps changing. You ask yourself, "Who I am now?" This loss of identity and **sense of self** is hard to comprehend because all this just happens in your face without your consent, as you never volunteered to be who you are now.

Spiritual Identity

This has a lot to do with the faith or congregation you belong to. Were you going to a church because of your husband or it was your choice? In some cultures when you get married you must go to the congregation where the in-laws belong to. If that was the case, then what happens when you remarry? You must change again especially if the new man belongs to a different church or religion? For men, they don't have to go through this. Women whether widowed or divorced it's the same. When my younger brother died in 2019, his wife was not very well supported by her congregation. They were not there for her morally as she had expected. She was in a dilemma whether to continue going to that same church or find another church that was going to be more welcoming to widows. Another change in spiritual identity will happen again. I thank God, my congregation from the Salvation Army, stood by me through and true.

Financial Identity

The loss of a spouse has a huge impact on household income. From two or three incomes down to one income. For me, it was from three incomes to a single income. My husband had an engineering company that he had just started and although it was not fully-fledged at least we were getting some income from it. When he died, I had no idea how to continue running that company.

His business partner decided to buy my husband out. This did not go as well as I had envisioned. I did not get much out of this. They had taken a loan from the bank to fund the new machinery they had purchased. My income remained the same, but it had to be spread over a bigger area now, to cover the daily expenses. I could not count on his pension as this was going to take some time to be paid out, and still, that loan from the bank for the company had to be paid.

I had to find a way of making extra income. I started doing dressmaking on a bigger scale. Before, I was only making clothes for my family as a hobby.

I would make clothes and my son would go around the community with his bike to deliver orders and pick up the payments. I was making clothes for the whole family, wedding dresses and bridesmaids dresses.

Since I was a lecturer, I worked Monday to Friday half day. Then people in my community knew me as the famous fashionable tailor who could dress up her family in exclusive outfits. I would make outfits just from a picture or the TV and combine different styles to come up with one outfit. In the end, I stopped buying my own clothes, made my own unique outfits. This is how I would advertise any new styles or fashion. Most people would place orders for clothes after they see me wearing them.

This gave me some extra income to help send my eldest daughter to boarding school. I remember my dad had moved in with us, and he would watch TV, make me a cup of tea, keep me company, while I was busy on my sewing machine. My younger sister Priscilla, who is also a widow, was very good at beading, so she helped me with beading the motifs that I used on the wedding dresses. Mavis is my younger sister who comes immediately after me, she was also good at sewing zippers. Mavis is also a widow; she would come every weekend to help me to install the difficult zippers on most male trousers or pants. It became a team effort and we all got some income out of this.

Outlook Identity

Your outlook is affected big time. This is the way you look at yourself and the way people look at you. You are no longer the same person, no matter how hard you try to block this out of your mind. It is what it is. You may pretend to be happy on the outside, but inside you are a total and complete pile of rubble. Your heart and feelings are broken into pieces. This will take time to repair and heal. I felt negative, jaded and wounded. It took me time to recover believe me. I was unable to engage with the same people that I was friends with before my husband passed. This is because our worlds had changed, and the view of their world was totally opposite to mine. This changed my identity once again.

You might say that Rose so what am I going to do with this information? What you must bear in mind is, you will never be the same person, with the same identity as before the loss of your spouse. The way you perceive the world and the way the world perceives you are totally strange to you. The only thing for you to be able to survive is to accept the fact that you are now a changed person with new identities. That alone will help you to start finding who you are, moving forward.

As human beings, we do not take change very well. Sometimes we are very resistant to change, trying to protect our old self. I'm sure most of you when you got married, you thought you had your life figured out, right? Surprise and changes happened unexpectedly, and your life is totally the opposite of what you had dreamt it to be.

The take from this is that you will remain the same wife to your husband, the same mother to your children, and the same daughter to your parents. Moving forward, you will now need to think about who you are when you approach the world in general. All these changes in your identity will need you to accept them, then find ways to work with them to move forward. You will have to take some time to work at rebuilding your **sense of self**, as you put the new pieces and what's left of the old self together, to form your new identity.

Reinventing yourself

Finding who you are, after trauma can be as taxing as going through grief. Just living with the title widow, is daunting enough. That life is coupled with frustrations, exhausting, painful emotions, heartaches, brand new widow tasks, as well as other responsibilities that will continue to pop up, none stop. Amid all this, you still must find out who you really are. Having walked this route myself, I know how bumpy this road can be. It must be walked not by anyone else, but by yourself. This will liberate you in the long run when you know who you are, as this will help you to face the world with the right perspective.

Knowing yourself means that you need to have a clear knowledge of your strengths and weaknesses, your dreams and desires as well as your fears and passions. Do you still remember what you like and don't like? What about what you can tolerate (endurance), your limitations, do you even have a purpose in life anymore? I guess if you remain naïve to this, then you are going to remain as confused as the day you got the news of your husband's passing!

Remember you are your own rescue.

"We have thoughts, but we are not our thoughts; Our thoughts are a part of who we are. We feel emotions, but we are not our emotions; emotions are a part of who we are. We have a body, but we are not our bodies; our body is a part of who we are. Our soul lies beneath all of these things; our soul's essence is the truth of who we are. It binds all of these aspects of us together." (Hay House Energy Healing)

As a human being, you need to bear in mind that every small thing you do, every role you play, every experience you go through, the alignment of your personalities is only part of who you wholly are. We must remember that we are human **BE-ings,** not human **DO-ings**. So, what we do should not define who we are. This is complicated right? It gets easier as we continue. Our identities are also changed because of the labels we give ourselves or those that people around us give us. This role you are playing as a widow has truly turned your world upside down but is that who you truly are on the inside. Ask yourself if everything we have talked about, identities are removed from you, what remains? Is that **YOU?**

To get to know yourself you must ask yourself these questions:

-

- What is your personality like?
- What are your dreams?
- What are your core values?
- What are your likes and dislikes?
- Do you still remember that you have a body and are you taking care of it?

What Is Your Personality?

You have a wide variety of information about your personality that you have collected over the years before and after you become a divorcee or a widow. You have a personality for the public to see and then the personality when you are behind closed doors. What you need to know now is among all those life's myriad of situations what really makes you react in a certain way? Many a time you have asked yourself, "Why did I do that?" Do you ever wonder what your character traits are? Are you the same person among your friends, family as well as strangers? What does the world see of you? Does your personality change on your good or bad days?

What Are Your Dreams?

Your dreams can build your future. Just because you a now a widow or divorcee, it does not mean you suddenly don't have any dreams anymore. Your dreams are your formula in creating and building your future. There is something that tells you that your life will not be this way forever. There are things you wanted to be from childhood that you probably had put on hold because you got married. What is it, or what are they? This should be the big part of your life now, rediscovering yourself. Do not be scared to share them with your children, or family and friends; as they might help those dreams come true.

What Are Your Core Values?

Core values are your fundamental beliefs. These are the guiding principles that will dictate your behavior and can help you to understand the difference between right and wrong. Core values are those values that you never compromise no matter what. This could be in your job, home, or every other aspect of your life. These core values could be integrity, honesty, flexibility, loyalty over excellence or vice versa. Is it ambition over responsibility, or improvement over innovation, could it be learning and wisdom, having fun or dedication to work? These core values affect the way you will make your decisions moving forward. These core values also affect your day to day living, communication, the influence you have in your family and the world. To succeed in your new life, you need to look closely at these core values. My question to you is, have your core values changed since you had been married and now that you are a widow or divorcee?

What Are Your Likes and Dislikes?

Knowing what you like, and dislike will make you secure in yourself. It gives you self-confidence, boosts your self-esteem and increases your self-worth. Ask yourself, what makes you happy? This is all about you. You must be selfish and look at you alone. You could have been doing somethings to please other people and have bitten your tongue a couple of times because you wanted to say NO but could not. It's time for you to learn to say NO and mean it. Do not compromise your happiness just to make other people enjoy theirs while you bleed inside. I spoke about the energy drainers and energy givers in the previous chapter. So which group do you associate with the most? That will determine your happiness too.

Do You Know Your Body?

Your body is your temple given to you by God. If you mess around with your body, it will mess you up big time. You must know how to take care of it. What makes it comfortable and what makes it thrive? Since you were born your body has continued to grow and change and sometimes it can disappoint and sometimes it can surprise you too. For women, our bodies change drastically soon after conceiving and progress after giving birth. When you reach menopause another big hump again. So, it does not matter where you are in age, the question is, do you know your body, are you taking good care of it? Do you love yourself enough to take self-care very seriously? Do you still bash yourself every time you look in the mirror?

In order to know and love your body here are things that should be on your priority list of taking care of your body.

- Self-love and self-care
- How much sleep do you get?
- What do you feed your body?
- How much exercise do you get?
- How much social and work life do you have? Are you lonely?

12

SELF LOVE

I f someone would ask you to marry yourself would that be a big YES or a NO?

If the answer is "Yes," then you don't have much do to in this section, but if the answer is "NO," then you have a lot to work on. A lot has happened in your life, do you still remember who you are and how to love yourself? You must know yourself as you will be with yourself for the rest of your life. Love the relationship that you have with yourself, so you can be able to love others. Love begins with loving ourselves and once we have enough, and our cup is overflowing then we can be able to share what is overflowing with others. You must know yourself, so you can love yourself too. I think it makes perfect sense.

Self-love is giving priority to your own well-being and happiness. **Self-love** means taking care of your own needs and not sacrificing your well-being to please others. **Self-love** is not settling for less than **you** truly deserve. Self-love is putting you first and not compromising your happiness to make other people happy. Self-love is not scaring yourself with wild and negative thoughts. Self-love is not bashing yourself with negative comments about how ugly you are. Self-love is having this beautiful image about yourself and expecting the best for yourself. Self-love is forgiving yourself for letting yourself down.

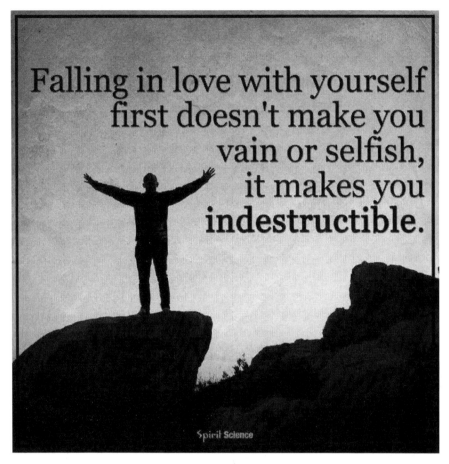

Falling in love with yourself first doesn't make you vain or selfish, it makes you indestructible.

Spirit Science

We are born alone and when we die, we die alone too. So, we need to love ourselves a lot. Loving yourself will create a firm foundation for you to face the cruel world out there. I love myself, more than before. I no longer care when people say that I am full of myself. Let them talk, they will get used to the new me. When I am full of myself then it means I will have some of me overflowing to share with everyone.

Ask yourself if you can still spend just an hour with yourself without driving yourself nuts. Do you freak yourself out when you are alone? Some people cannot stand the idea of being alone with themselves. Can you listen to your own breathing at all or you surround yourself with distracting loud music, that you have no idea how you breathe? How can you take care of others when you cannot even know how you breathe? You are the captain of your body.

How do you experience self-love?

1. Self-love is the **cornerstone** of your healing process. It will give you confidence in yourself, knowing that you can still love and be there for yourself no matter what. It will boost your energy and your insight into transforming your life. Life will not feel like a chore when you love yourself. Self-love will help you to connect with the real you and help you to let go of any anger and regrets that you might still be hanging on to.

2. **Anger and regrets** are like cancer that continue to eat you slowly and before you know it, your whole inside is gone. When you practice self-love, you will be able to ask yourself whether the pity party life is really what you want or not. Crying about the problems and not taking any action is not a good way to love yourself. To me, it's a self-induced destructive behavior.

3. When you love yourself, you **do not scare** yourself out of your skin. You see people watching scary movies that they know will give them goosebumps, or nightmares for the rest of the week. They still watch it anyway. You also do not allow your mind to continue thinking about the horror stories that you heard. How many times do you go to bed thinking of these horror stories you heard people talking about during the day? I had this habit of thinking of the worst happening to me every time I fell ill. I would visualize myself dying and my kids being orphans. The more I thought about it, the worse my health got. Quit doing that to yourself. Remember every time you think of negative and frightening thoughts; you are creating negative affirmations in your life. The same way you create those negative thoughts in your mind is the same way you can create positive thoughts and affirmations in your mind.

4. Keep **negativity** out of your life. It is very exhausting. Staying around people that are always complaining about how hard life is, how poor

they are, how their in-laws have treated them badly, but not doing anything to correct the situation is very toxic. I did that for the longest while, thinking that it was normal to be hanging around people that wallowed in their sorrows like me. I soon found out that it did nothing but drain my energy with nothing positive coming out of it. I had also reached a point that this widowhood journey was like a curse. Sometimes it just needs you to look over the fence for a solution.

5. Self-love means not focusing on the **pain of the wounds** caused by the loss of your husband or relationship. It means looking at the ways you can heal and make a fresh start. When you are hurting don't look at the future through that veil of pain. You must learn to think positively. You have the power to control your thoughts, so you can stop those negative and painful thoughts to keep occupying space in your mind. I learned the hard way, after letting the wounds control my life. I had multiple health issues and I had to let go of the painful past and my health bounced back in no time. You can do the same too.

6. Stop **criticizing yourself**. When you have done something wrong to yourself or to other people, be gentle with yourself. If you cannot be gentle with yourself, how can you expect other people to be gentle with you? Think of all the bashing that you have thrown at yourself. That's self-inflicted pain. When you look in the mirror what do you see? Do you love what you see or is it your worst expression of yourself that you see? As women, we are very critical of our image. "Oh, I hate my legs, they are too fat. I hate my lips they are too small; my butt is too big or too small." There is always something wrong with our bodies. Now it's the best time for you to find at least five things that you love about your body. If there are other parts you don't like, get them fixed, go to the gym or get Botox. If you don't have money to change that then let's get back to the drawing board, learn to love what you have. You know when we learn to eat right, exercise and get enough sleep, our bodies will work with us not against us.

7. What is your **philosophy**? What are your **beliefs**? You can change those beliefs if they are making you miserable. If you are not happy

with your life, then you have a chance to change it. When you love yourself, that creates a good foundation for you, when you decide to remarry. Do not wait for other people to make you happy, you must love yourself enough to make yourself happy. Connect with your inner self in order to know who you are and what makes you happy.

8. How often do you **laugh** at yourself or find humor in your mistakes? Some days, just watch funny movies that make you laugh your socks off. It releases all the stress. Find some comedy movies that you share with friends or even with your kids and laugh like no one is watching. Dance to some music in the shower, in your car and while cleaning your house. I have this habit of blasting my music in my car and dance with my head while singing along in my car. It helps me to destress after a long day at work. Don't mind people looking at you, wave at them and give them a big smile and they will laugh with you.

9. Wear **clothes** that make you feel sexy, happy and comfortable. Don't follow fashion simply because everyone is doing it while you are compromising your happiness and freedom. Are you buying items that are running down your budget to impress other people or to belong to a group of people? It can also be that you are way back in fashion and your style is so outdated you look like you are from the '60s. At least wear something that's more recent in the fashion trend.

10. **Don't blame your parents for the dysfunctional life that they exposed you to. That's all they knew at that time when they raised you. Remember people behave according to the information that they have, at that time. You have a choice to stay in that self-pity lane or change into a better life lane.**

11. Don't **label** yourself with other people's opinions of you. People will always talk about you, no matter what you do or don't do. So be yourself and love yourself more. No one besides you will ever love you the way you are supposed to be loved. They might call you crazy because you are fighting for your children and your welfare. Tell them that they haven't seen crazy yet, as more is coming. On the other side of the coin, if what people are saying has some truth in it, then change whatever

needs to be changed otherwise you could risk losing some people in your life.

12. Set healthy **boundaries** to protect your heart and emotions. This will help to nurture your heart and build strong relationships around you. Setting healthy boundaries is also allowing yourself to say NO when you are not in alignment with whatever has been demanded of you. Healthy and firm boundaries will make people treat you with respect. One thing to remember is never to move your boundaries in order to please other people, while it's killing you inside. Healthy boundaries will also help you not to hang around negative people and toxic people. Boundaries will also keep the energy drainers away from you, as they will know that their manipulative habits are not allowed. Healthy boundaries will also remind you not to let negative comments from people get to you. Remember when a person hurts you, they are just trying to get you to keep them company in their pity party zone. Acknowledge them and tell them you have moved on; you are on a healing journey and you don't intend to hang out with them anymore.

13. Be kind and gentle to yourself. Stop blaming yourself for the mistakes you have made in the past. Stop sending yourself on all these guilt trips when you cannot control situations in your life. Learn to say NO. Let's learn to declutter our minds at the end of each day by doing either yoga, going to the gym, or take a walk to get some fresh air. Take some deep breaths, close your eyes and release whatever tension that might have built up in your muscles. As you breathe out, tell yourself, "I love you. This too will pass, and I am going to be alright."

14. Stop comparing yourself to other people. You are unique in your own way. I used to ask myself why I ended up as a widow? Why did God not give me a sign that this was going to happen maybe I would have left to go to another place? Life is full of surprises and it is how we react to those surprises or embrace them is what matters. Comparison is a thief of joy. You will forever ask yourself why things happened the way they did. Most of the time you will never get a response.

15. Learn to praise yourself for every small step you take towards your goals

or your healing journey. Now I always tell myself that am wonderful, sexy, fabulous, intelligent, powerful, and beautiful. This is called practicing **infinite intelligence**. The more you say it to yourself, the more your mind starts to believe it, and it becomes a reality to you.

16. When you love yourself, you get support when you need it. You do not suffer in silence when help is everywhere no matter how embarrassing the situation is. There are support groups everywhere with like-minded people. If you are not sure, ask. Network with other people to get new ideas and avoid being lonely and isolated in your house or room.

17. Use the mirror to help you to love and forgive yourself. Look yourself in the mirror and tell yourself:

18. *"I love you no matter what life throws at me. I know that I am going through this journey of healing from my past, but everything will be okay. I am a fighter and I will win this battle."*

19. When you tell yourself this looking in the mirror, helps you to see what your eyes are telling you. Usually, your eyes do not lie to you. It becomes a reality.

Remember love begins with you. When your heart is full of love for yourself, only then can you have a heart for others. Having self-love will make you closer to God, as God is Love. If the world turns against you, remember that your God will always have unconditional love for you! Lack of self-love usually results in this "big ego" that is a sign of no self-love for yourself and those around you.

What is self-care?

When I talk about self-care, it's not only about self-indulgence or pampering yourself. It's all about understanding that you are worth a lot, you have value as a human being, and you have the right to treat yourself accordingly. As women, we very good at nurturing others, but always put ourselves at the end of the line. As a mother and a wife, you take care of your family when they are sick, but you always forget to care for yourself in the process.

Read literature to grow your mind

This can help widen your horizon, and learn new things that help you go out of your comfort zone. You must find the right books that you know you will learn something new from and grow as a person. When I came to North America I went back to University and got new qualifications to align myself with my new goals.

CREATE YOUR OWN SPA AND TAKE CARE OF YOURSELF

Photo Credit: https://www.healthista.com

Create your own girl (s) retreat to pamper yourself.

Women generally never take time off for themselves. You can create this loving space for yourself in your own home or go out on weekends with the girls. I started doing this. I would go for weekend prayer retreats with other women in my church. This gave me time to unwind and rejuvenate my tired brain. I loved this time away from home with other productive women. It also made see what I was missing out in life, in the normal world.

Test Drive Your Dream Car

How do you feel about test driving that red convertible sports car? Have fun test driving your dream car at your nearest car dealership. The salesman cannot force you to buy the car anyways. Enjoy that feeling with the wind blowing your hair, wow, what a feeling! Own that time, you deserve it.

That could be you enjoying that ride in your dream car for FREE!!!

Photo Credit: Suparna Dutt D'Cunha in Asia

Writing for healing and self-care

Use writing to put down all your wounds, frustrations and your deepest secrets on paper. Writing helps you to release all your emotions from your flustered mind. This will create more space in your mind, for more logical thinking and purges all the negativity onto paper. You can use collages to purge your mind, it works the same way too. The good thing about writing or collages is there is no one to judge you. When you have done this, you can either burn notes or throw them away where you never see them again. This is like you are telling your mind, "Out of sight, out of mind." When done well, this will help you not to dwell on those wounds, as well as help you to heal.

Photo Credit: alamy.com

Spend Time Outdoors

Walking in nature is liberating. It's such a good feeling to smell the grass and hear the birds singing. Take some time to just unwind. I usually try to walk barefooted on the grass just to get myself grounded. Walking in nature helps you to recharge your batteries.

Be your authentic self

As humans, we have this tendency of trying to belong or identify with a certain group of people, when in fact we are killing ourselves inside silently. Being authentic to yourself is being able to speak your mind in a respectful way. I call this **Mob Psychology** when you go with the flow whether it's good for you or not, just because you want to belong to a group. Let people see you and love you for who you are. You do you and let others do themselves.

Look at Your Accomplishments in Life

This is like a gratitude list. What have you accomplished so far for yourself? You might think because you got married and you ended up as a widow or a divorcee, it makes you a failure. NO. Change that thought to a powerful positive thought. At least you got married and you walked down the aisle. Some people are dying to have what you have. You cannot control what happened to the relationship after you said I DO.

Positive Self-Talk

As humans, we have no idea what **self-talk** can do to our lives. This is the inner voice in your mind that says things quietly to you. Negative self-talk tends to make you miserable and steal your joy as well as have a negative impact on your health. If you continue to tell yourself that you will never get well. This will become reality for sure because that is what your brain will start molding as reality into your life. You are talking to your mind and telling it what to do. The brain is very obedient as it will take that information, store it and then use it for you or against you. Let's be mindful of what we say to ourselves. Use **Self-talk** to encourage yourself when you feel you are not performing at your best in life.

Self-esteem

Self-esteem is how you feel about yourself. How you think of yourself while comparing yourself to others. Do you feel like you are not good enough or beautiful enough to find someone else to love you? Self-esteem is not something from within us. It is something from outside ourselves that will influence how we feel at any given time. This will affect how we interpret the opinions of others about ourselves.

Signs of Healthy Self-Esteem

You probably have a good sense of who you are if you show the following signs:

- Confidence
- Ability to say no
- Ability to express your needs
- Positive outlook
- Ability to see overall strengths and weaknesses and accept them
- Negative experiences don't impact your overall perspective

Signs of low self-esteem

You may need to work on how you perceive yourself if you exhibit any of these signs of poor self-esteem:

- Negative outlook
- Lack of confidence
- Inability to express your needs
- Focus on your weaknesses
- Excessive feelings of shame, depression, or anxiety
- A belief that others are better than you
- You cannot accept positive feedback
- Extensive fear of failure

Having low self-esteem means you think low of yourself and you always look down on yourself. You view yourself as an underachiever all the time and not good enough to do anything. Having high self-esteem gives you more confidence as you believe in yourself. Having high self-esteem boosts your morale as you look at the world with a positive perspective and you feel you can tackle what life throws at you. High self-esteem means you do not have to seek approval from others to feel good about yourself. When you have high self-esteem, you don't look at your faults, you focus more on your accomplishments/successes. Self-criticism is the worst enemy of your self-esteem.

Self-worth

Self-worth is a direct measure of how you value and regard yourself despite what other people might think of you. Self-worth is not easily affected by external factors or how circumstances change. I always think of my role model, Tina Turner. She knew she was worth much more than what her husband at the time Ike, was giving her. She left him and she was homeless and poor for some time but look at what came out of it all. So, had she ignored her self-worth we would not be talking about this today. Having a high level of self-worth means that you have a favorable opinion of yourself. It also means have an unshakable faith in yourself and in your ability to get things done. You are worthy of great things. You put yourself first and others second. You know what self-love is and have high-level self-esteem. No matter what people say about you in a negative way, you will know deep down that you are worth much, much, more than gold. It means no matter the circumstances you will remain steadfast to your true self. It also means that you believe in yourself that your opinion of yourself is the only one that is going to shake or move you. This also strengthens your **self-power**.

Mix Up Your Life

Don't make your life a routine you are too young for that boring, structured and rigid routine. If you were used to a certain route going home, change it a little if it won't take you off course. If you were used to eating certain foods, try a new diet. You can also change your look, your clothes, and your hair. You can even change up the furniture in your house starting with the bedroom and see how this works for you.

Your Happiness

Do not put conditions on your happiness, by putting your happiness on hold until you get what you want in life. Don't compromise your happiness on small things in life. Your happiness is the cornerstone. Of your life and your health. When you are happy you don't put your life on Autopilot. You know your purpose in life and you also remain on track with your goals.

Remember:

"You cannot change how people feel about you, so don't try. Just live your life and be happy". Unknown

I believe happiness is a choice that you make as an individual.

How Much Sleep Do You Get?

A good night's sleep is a gateway to a healthy and productive day. Lack of sleep affects your energy levels during the day, emotional balance and even your weight.

Tips on how to get a great night sleep

- How many power naps do you take during the day? How long are they? If they go past 20mins, then they are not power naps anymore. If these naps are causing you to lose your sleep at night, then discontinue them totally.
- Make sure your room is dark and use heavy dark drapes to cover your blinds. You can also use a sleep mask to cover your eyes.
- Avoid any bright screens in the room 1-2 hours before bedtime. Use the night lamps in your room and bathrooms so that you do not turn on the overhead or side lamps at night when you use the washroom.
- Get some exercise during the day as this improves the symptoms for insomnia, sleep apnea and it helps the length of time you get a deep restful sleep during your sleep. Exercise elevates your metabolism and helps with your weight. Make sure you exercise 3 hours before bedtime to give your body time to unwind.
- Watch what you eat before bedtime. Limit the amount of caffeine and nicotine before bedtime. Smoking is a stimulant that can disrupt your sleep a whole lot.
- Don't eat a big meal two hours before going to bed. No high spicy and acidic foods that can cause stomach troubles and heartburn.
- Don't drink too many liquids before bedtime as this will increase your trips to the washroom which will disrupt your sleep big time.
- Eating too many sweets, refined carbs like white bread, white rice and pasta will cause wakefulness at night and causes your body to lose the restorative stages of sleep.
- Wind down and clear your head before your bedtime. Going to bed

angry usually keeps me awake at night as I toss and turn the whole night. So, until I fix whatever is bothering me, I will not sleep well. Anger is a big cause of sleepless nights. Visualize going to a restful place and imagine that place being as calming as possible. Just focusing on you being relaxed and how this makes you feel. Deep breathing in and out.

- You can also read a very boring book or watch a boring movie that will send you to sleep right away.
- Check the environment of your bedroom or your bedroom or your sleeping area. What are the temperatures? They should be around the standard recommended temperatures which are 65 degrees Fahrenheit or 18-degree Centigrade. When you go to sleep the body temperature decrease. But that does not mean you put your heating full blast to keep you warm at night. You can put on socks on your feet or use a hot water bottle to warm up the bed. Some people use electric blankets that you can regulate the heat. Never make your bedroom a courtroom, where you settle all the household issues.
- Keep the noise down. A quiet room is more conducive to better sleep than a noisy place. You can mask the noise with a fan running in your bedroom. Some people use earplugs, but for me, I get petrified of what if there is a fire and you cannot hear the fire alarm. So be mindful of that if you decide to use earplugs. Most people use earplugs on a long overnight flight so they can get a restful sleep.
- Stop worrying about life issues before bedtime.

What you feed your body is also self-care

Weight Control

- You are what you eat! Following a good diet boosts your immune system and increases your energy levels. Eating a healthy diet and regular exercise also helps you improve your cardiovascular health. You might say you don't have money for the gym, but you can do some exercises at home to help your body to stay active and in shape. Plan at least 30 mins a day for some physical exercises. You can take a walk in the park or in your neighborhood. You can use the stairs to help with the physical exercises as well. Try and have a balanced diet daily.

- Have at least five servings of fruits and vegetables in a day. Check the calories on the food labels when you go grocery shopping. Cut down on sodas, fruit juices as they have high levels of sugar. Eat lean meats like fish and turkey, even lean beef and chicken breast. If you decide to eat other parts of the chicken, then remove the skin, as this contains all fat in the chicken.
- Try and have breakfast daily as this helps to lower your blood sugar.
- You will feel better about your appearance when you eat a healthy diet. Once you feel good about your appearance this will elevate your confidence, self-worth, and self-esteem as well.

Improves your mood

- A good diet increases the production of endorphins in your brain. These are the brain cells that leave you feeling happy and more relaxed. When you feel happy you will feel better in the long run.

Fights diseases

- A healthy diet helps to combat common diseases like, diabetes, heart disease, and stroke and helps to keep the bad cholesterol at bay. Diseases like cardiovascular diseases, arthritis, acne, and gout, are some diseases that can be prevented.
- This is not something you can change overnight you can gradually watch what you eat depending on your staple foods. Stay away from junk foods as much as you can.
- How much water are you drinking?

Are you worrying excessively?

If you are a person that is always living on the edge with the "what ifs" on her mind.

What if **I get sick?** What if **I don't have enough money for the** kid's school fees? What if **I am not good enough**?

You have not even tried it yet and already your mind is running away from you. Take a step back, look at the issue if you can control it. If you can, then work on the solution if not then look for an alternative. I have learned that worrying about something without doing something about it is a total waste of time.

Excessive worrying can cause a: -

Nervous breakdown, Increased anxiety levels,

High blood pressure, IBS irritable bowel syndrome,

Nausea, Fatigue,

Aches and pains in the body, Depression.

Sometimes worry is a good thing as it prepares you for things to come. If the worrying is paralyzing you and stealing all your joy, then it's very unhealthy. It needs to be stopped.

How to fix the worry habit

1. Take note of all the issues that are worrying, bugging you or that keep you in the worry zone.
2. See if you can find solutions to those issues then you have nothing to worry about, take some action to solve the problems. Do you still remember the Serenity Prayer we spoke about earlier in the book?

Serenity Prayer

Lord give me the
serenity to
Accept

The things I
cannot change.
The courage to change the things I can
And wisdom to know
The difference.

So, worrying about things that you have no control over although easy, is unproductive worrying. Learn to have productive worrying where you are looking for solutions.

13

FINDING LOVE AGAIN

D on't break your own heart by dating without healing properly. Putting band-aids on your hurts without cleaning the wounds and going through the healing process authentically, for the wounds to heal, makes you guilty of cheating on your true self. You are deceiving the new partner coming into your life, making him think that you are whole when you are an empty shell inside. You become a whole person when you are authentic to yourself by having your whole-self truly healed.

Ask yourself, since the funeral for your spouse what steps have you taken to heal your heart? It does not matter in which order you took them. If you feel you need to redo the whole healing process, please do so. If you still feel angry about the passing of your spouse then you need to heal some more. You owe it to the new person coming into your life to be emotionally available for them too. Suppressing your hurts will turn you into a vicious volcano waiting to erupt at any time.

I know that thinking of going back into the dating pond again is nerve-racking. There is a feeling of being under a microscope. Your every move is examined by friends and relatives, coworkers who can post your life on social media to entertain themselves. They want to see if you are behaving properly, are you mourning and grieving accordingly? Do you seem like you are too excited to find someone to replace their relative, friend, their son or their dad? What are you posting on social media? I know that sometimes as a widow you can get paranoid about these things. I have realized that worrying about what people will say about what you are doing will not change the status of a widow. You must make decisions based on what you see fit for your life and your children. Remember that you have no control over what people can say or think about your life.

When you are ready to date you will be able to accept the loss of your spouse without any duress. You will find that you will be more interested in getting to know the other person, to share your love, family, finances, fears, and happiness, not just to be laid, but also to have a life with this new man. You will also realize that the ripple effect from the waves of grief will grow smaller and smaller.

You will not forget to be respectful to all the people in your late husband's life as well. They also are going through loss, so you cannot wave this dating issue in their face like you are glad that he is gone and now you can find someone else.

I am sure you want to go into a happy and long-term relationship, but you must do some final clean-up of your house. Is there some laundry that needs to be cleaned up in your heart, mind, and emotions that you are still holding onto? These are what I call, the **silent killers** of your future relationships. Everyone has some baggage they carry around. You now must take a closer look to see what might destroy the new relationships in any way. You have gone through hell and back. The trauma has changed the person whom everyone used to know. Without fighting the trauma, look at how it has molded you into this strong independent person.

Can you marry yourself at this point? Are your emotions all over the place? This is not the time to run for the hills and think that those issues will suddenly wake up gone. Ask yourself what it is that makes you not want to marry yourself? There must be bad issues or scars that make you to not be in a relationship with you. You probably want to be jumping from one relationship to the other, in the high hopes of finding the love that you are dying to get. I'm sure the last thing you want is to be deeply discouraged when the same old problems start to pop up and destroy your future relationships.

So, try it out and see if you are comfortable with dating again. If not, there is no hurry, wait until you are ready. You will notice that the more you go out on dates the more comfortable you will get.

The emotional baggage checklist

- You still have the damaged goods syndrome. You still feel like you are not worthy to be loved and to love again.
- You still sound like a broken record replaying arguments, fights, or breakups you had from your previous relationship(s) in your mind.
- Do you still have insecurity, intimacy issues, or the fear of being vulnerable again?
- Do you have some unresolved feelings of love from your late spouse and other previous relationship that need closure?
- Trust issues are still flooding your mind every time you think of getting into another romantic relationship?
- Do you still have flashbacks of painful memories of all the people that hurt you during the widowhood journey that you have not forgiven yet?

Set yourself free from the bondage

1. Accept your past for what it is: This is the time to make peace with your past before you start dating again. You must be brutally honest with yourself now.
2. Pay close attention to any doubts: Is your mind saying one thing and your heart another? You don't want anyone saying this to you, "I told you so." Take note of every little thing.
3. Plan your strategy: Now that you have your final list of the issues compiled, you need to find out how you will overcome them. If you cannot deal with them then get a coach, a pastor or a mentor to help you with them. It might just take some prayers to overcome those struggles. It's all up to you to see what works with you, depending on what it is that needs to be straightened.

I have heard some people say that, in order to get over a man, you need to get under another man as soon as possible. It does not work like that in the real world. I cannot say this enough, don't put a timeline to this healing process. Go through this process with an open heart.

You also need to know that it's not the emotional baggage that's the biggest issue here. It is how you will handle and relate to the emotional baggage. I have since learned that nothing should steal my joy unless I give it consent to happen. If going for a walk, jogging, singing, dancing, screaming in the shower or in your car for some hours helps you, then go for it.

Let me give you an example: -

Let's say you are walking in the dark in your house, you walk into a coffee table and you hit your pinky toe. Ouch, it hurts. You start to curse the table, calling it names, jumping up and down or blaming other people for putting the table there. But it's not the table's fault, you are the one that walked into it, in the dark. So now it's how you will react to this pain that matters. In this case, you are cursing at everyone in the house. Is it the people's fault that you did not switch on the light or there is something else beyond that?

This is what happens when you have suppressed your wounds and pain for some time. When one little thing happens, we are quick to blame shift it onto others and not looking at the real issue. You never looked at you, but everyone else. It's never your fault, but everyone else's. Learn to take responsibility for your own actions.

Now that you are going back into the dating world after a long dry painful spell, it is hard as things change fast. You probably have no idea where to start, how people around you are going to react once you tell them that you want to start dating again. You might have no clue what to expect. Are you scared of being intimate with another man again? I am hoping that you are not expecting this new guy to fix the problems that you have carried over from your previous life. You might be worried about how you will behave on your first date. Go through the chapter on how to love yourself, again. Just remind yourself that, "You are beautiful." Tell yourself, "I love you." Once you can love yourself again, you can love someone else. Don't wait for this other new person to validate you and tell you that you are beautiful. Don't get me wrong. It's important that he tells you that you are beautiful. But you must tell yourself that and accept it too.

Remind yourself that you are the best thing that ever happened to you. I tried it; it works. Now I tell myself all the time how beautiful I look and how great I am. I look in the mirror and tell myself, "You hot, sexy, beautiful, curvy mama, you rock!!" That makes me feel on top of the world and I leave my house feeling like a million bucks with a huge spring in my step, accompanied by a big smile! Now I run my life the way I feel and comfortable with. No one is able to take you out of the self-bashing hole more than yourself. Don't fall into that same routine that most people fall into, after going through trauma. They don't work on themselves and get into relationships with some unfinished business from their past. The healing process is a continuous process, the more you become aware of the need to continue loving yourself, the more you will let go of all the baggage.

You need to be aware that we all have a past that has caused emotional turmoil in our lives. **Know it, own it, and process it**. If you cannot do it alone then find help. Remember there is nothing that you cannot undo if you put your mind to it.

When the emotional baggage creeps back in, ask yourself:

1. Is this issue new or old?
2. What's new about this problem?
3. How can I take care of myself in this situation?

Everyone wants to love and to be loved although in a different way. Some people heal faster than others. So, don't compare yourself with others. Ask yourself what you still need to do to prepare yourself for the world out there?

Going through the trauma of your loss, it's tough. You might find that some people, especially the in-laws, they will start to validate your pain. It's time for you to start validating your loss yourself. It happened and nothing can change that, and you can never be over that loss, but you will heal through learning to live with the pain. Stop assessing how much damage the trauma caused in your life, learn and grow from it. It does not matter how you continue to wallow in your grief, your tears will never be acknowledged by anyone, except yourself and your children. The healing process is very comforting, and it will help you to move on with your life without feeling or being sent on a guilt trip by family and friends. You will see that you will learn to be compassionate to yourself.

Bear in mind that you still have a choice in all this. Wouldn't you want to date a person who is also starting on a clean slate, with neither of you expecting the other to be their Counselor or Coach?

You were in a season that has passed with the death of your spouse or your ex. Its time you shed off that old skin and walk away from it and start a new life. It's time for you to wear some very dark glasses, to block out some E.Ds (Energy Drainers) from your life. Learn to confuse the devil too in the process. Surprise people with your new-found self. Things are not going to be smooth-running in this new life, but you must put a brave face and to hold your head high and move on. This is when you need to shift your self-Esteem, self-confidence, self-worth, self-love, self-awareness gears into drive mode. Remember that no storm lasts forever and behind that storm comes sunshine. Just keep pushing and you will soon get the life and relationship you wish for.

Some partners discuss what to do after the other is gone. Some people will discuss when to start dating. So, as the general public, we might not know what the two love birds had agreed on before either died. If a spouse has a terminal illness sometimes things like this can be discussed and people should not be quick to judge as we are not aware of what the couple discussed.

Let go of the victim mentality, the poor me mentality. Once you accept what happened, you will heal faster than denying and dwelling on it. You are the one that has chosen to move on and find love. Moving around with your head down and still feeling sorry for yourself only projects you as a needy and co-dependent person. Shake that victim mentality and you will feel confident and you will gain your power back from grief. Soon you will find yourself feeling confident again to be in the dating pond. If you still feel bogged down, then seek professional help from a coach or a therapist.

What kind of relationship are you looking for?

"Lots of people want to ride with you in the limo. But what you really need is someone who will help you catch the bus."
Oprah Winfrey

Here is another bone of contention. It is also very vital for you to think of the kind of relationship you are looking for. Love is not a one-size-fits-all. People choose to fall in love with different people for different reasons. So, what relationship does your situation fits into? It's wise to choose the one who is looking for the same things that you are searching for.

7 types of romantic relationships

- **Monogamous Relationships.** This is the most traditional relationship that most people lean towards. This is the one that is mostly understood by children who see it from their parents. This relationship calls for one sex or romantic partner at a time. One man for one woman and God for us all. Most civil marriages call for this type of marriage.
- **Polyamorous Relationships.** In this relationship, there is more than one romantic partner at a time. Polyamorous couples have a primary partner and a secondary partner. These partners can change their rankings accordingly. Effective and honest communication is a requirement so that these parties are all on the same page. Side Chick (Booty Call); In this situation, the guy always calls you last minute to hang out. He never takes you out during the day to public places. He is always busy during the day but wants to come over to your house around 2.00 am and tells you he misses you. Really, why at that time of the night? You are supposed to be in bed resting not responding to some loser who is lonely, wants to feed his sexual appetite and his ego. Don't answer the call unless if that's the relationship you are looking

for my dear. He might tell you that he can't sleep because something is bothering him, and he just wants your company. All he wants is the cookie from you. Once he gets what he came for, he will leave without any remorse. Is that what you want for yourself? You must be better than that.

- **Open Relationships.** In this relationship, both parties share physical intimacy with anyone they want. There is also some element of both the monogamous and polyamorous relationships. So, each person can have as many sexual partners as they want, but with only one romantic partner. How to know if your new guy wants to see other people:
- He will joke about it.
- He might have open fantasies about it.
- He might have the guts to introduce you to friends who love it. Open relationships are not for everyone. Don't ever feel pressured to be in this type of relationship just to be with this macho man with six or eight packed abdomen, or the Mr Handsome, rich and seemingly well put together. If you prefer the monogamous relationship, then don't agree to share your guy with anyone else.
- **Long Distance Relationships .** The partners in this relationship live far away from each other. This could be in different cities, provinces, states, countries or even continents. It works for some people that can make it work as the physical intimacy might be lacking in this type of relationship. The distance separates these couples, it might be hard to keep the fire burning unless frequent communication is kept alive in this relationship. Some couples might continue indefinitely as long-distance partners due to several reasons. I have also found out that there are other individuals that just look for cyber relationships, just to find someone to chat with when they are bored. So, check these individuals out to see how long they want this cyber relationship to go before you decide to meet face to face.
- **Casual Sex Relationships.** In this type of relationship, both partners agree to have sex with each other and there are no romantic relationship ties. There is no love in this relationship although both parties can

remain monogamous to each other. There is no emotional connection at all in this relationship.

- **Friends with Benefits.** There is an established platonic friendship in this relationship. It's like the casual sex relationship, which begins when these two friends agree to act on a mutual sexual attraction. This relationship can be kept going as long as both or one of the party's starts dating someone else.
- **Asexual Relationships.** In this relationship, the partners don't experience any sexual desires or attraction to others, although they still want to participate in a romantic relationship. There are some cases where an asexual person enters a relationship with a sexual person. The couple can choose to be sexless or the asexual partner can "compromise" by engaging in sex occasionally under agreed circumstances. Partners can experiment with "pseudosexual behavior," such as cuddling and spooning, to find an arrangement that works for both.

How to define the relationship you want

Don't be a volunteer victim to loneliness! Pray about this first so you can get some direction from the Lord. Ask God to help you on this journey. If he is taken you this far, then he can take you further. Prayer worked and still works for me. My widowhood journey was met with lots of tribulations. Sometimes I wonder how I managed to be here writing this book! I believe God had a purpose for me to go through what I went through so I can one day help many women around the world who are faced with the same adversaries. There is a God in heaven, he helped me to be where I am today.

1. **Are You Looking for Exclusivity?** Most people are comfortable with monogamous relationships. Make sure the relationship you will get into aligns with your desires and needs. Set clear expectations when you start the dating process. If you are looking for another type of relationship make sure the other party knows what you are looking for too. Set clear boundaries so that you are not found regretting being

in another type of relationship you do not agree with. Make sure that the guy is also on the same page with you. Never assume anything in a relationship. You might feel or assume he is ready to be exclusive. If you feel he is not ready, then he is not ready. He needs to say it and his actions need to match his words. Pay close attention to your gut feeling or even ask him and let him tell you what kind of relationship he is looking for. Sometimes he might beat about the bush about this topic, just make it clear what you are looking for.

2. **Quality Time with Your Partner.** Quality time with your partner is very crucial. You need that time to get to know each other. Are you a person who needs time alone to feel connected to your new man? If so, talk about this so he knows what is expected of him. Do you also love attention like too much lovey-dovey always? What is your love language and his love language?

3. **What Kind of Partner Are You Looking For?** How people love and want to be loved is different with everyone. The way you are loved and how you connect with the love languages is different for every individual too. You will need to talk about this too so both of you know how to love each other. Do you value quality time with your partner? Words of affirmation are these foreign to you? You need to express openly exactly what you are looking for, so there are no misconceptions about what you want. As human beings, we will try to show love to our partners based on how we want to be loved and this might not work with the other partner. Learn their love language and teach them yours.

4. **Share Your Religious and Political Choices** This should not wait until you are deep into the relationship. If your religion is very important to you, then you need to have someone who has the same beliefs as you. You might want to know about the different religious beliefs out there so you can see whether they go with what you can live with.

5. **Do You Have Career Goals?** If both of you have career goals, they need to be shared so that you can support each other's dreams. These career goals may also involve moving to another place, is this going to

be an issue with either of you or not? As a couple, you need to be on the same page. If children are involved, then you need to be clear about what might happen in the future.

6. **What Are Your Deal Breakers?** Is it cheating, religious beliefs, smoking, abuse or addictions of any kind? Share this so it's common knowledge to your partner. Are you conscious of your height? Are you comfortable with dating a guy shorter than you? Is a certain age a deal-breaker for you?

7. **Do You Want More Kids in This Relationship**? You must be on the same page on this. Surprises along the line, like wanting kids when the man does not like kids can be detrimental to the relationship. If both of you have children, then are you ready to have a blended family?

8. **Separated or Married Man** Never play a technical game with a man who is still married. He keeps telling you that he will divorce his wife and then elope with you. He might also say he is separated for a couple of months and is working on his divorce. Run for the hills, there is other fish in the pond, don't waste your time playing waiting games. The "what ifs," will then join you and talk to you in your sleep, because you have no guarantee that he will leave his wife for you! He is separated for a few months, unless if that marriage died years ago, but my advice is to stay away for these men as they are very unemotionally available for you. It's a tough call, to be honest. I have worked with some women who were caught up in this kind of situation. They end up wasting a lot of time with this guy and end up staying as a mistress in the relationship because the guy cannot get out of the marriage. So do your homework ladies before getting into any mess.

Now the question is, which relationship works for you? Are you looking to be married by common law, conjugal or a situational partnership? If you have children then you might think of having the children on board with this decision. The type of relationship you choose might affect their welfare. If you decide to be officially married, think of the widow's benefits if there is any. Once you get married you lose the widow's benefits for good. The children will continue to get theirs until they are 18 years. If this new guy, unfortunately, kicks the bucket again, you cannot get the pensions for both men, you can only get the pension for the last husband. Think about the health care benefits that you might be getting from your widow's package. So, you have some serious thinking to do here. I am not trying to scare you away from getting married again. I am just being a realist. Be very practical in approaching this situation especially if there are any children under the age of 17 years involved.

People might say you are concerned about the money issue only. I am just being realistic, and you need to be too. If the new man can support you or you can make it with the new man, I give you my blessings. For a relationship to work, you will need to have the financial side in good standing. You will need a solid love base and physical attraction to complete the puzzle.

If you are in doubt consult a lawyer, for a fee.

Loneliness: Inside and outside of a relationships

Now that you have decided to move on and find new love, it's a choice that you have made. You can come out of it if you decide to. This thing called **loneliness,** it has made a lot of people go into or stay in unhealthy relationships just so that they are not alone. After a while, you will get very lonely and you feel the need to have that pillow talk with someone. Loneliness usually creeps up on you and if it overstays its welcome, you might be vulnerable to suffering from the infamous Mr. Loneliness.

Let me tell you that even in romantic relationships, loneliness is very common, and this is the reason that many couples are breaking up or cheating on their spouses or partners. When your partner is not emotionally available in the relationship, it means they are not present in the relationship at all. They have other things to do with their time than spend quality time with their spouses. Even some children feel very lonely in their homes when they have both parents staying in the same house with them. It's all because these parents never have time to spend with their children. If the children do not get the love they need from their parents they will get somewhere else. Some will end up using drugs just to numb the loneliness or to feel accepted to a group of people.

When you do find this Mr. Nice guy, make sure you do not make him your hobby, subsequently losing your mind and forgetting that you have children that still need you. A lot of our young children now think that getting married is a waste of time because people will die young so what's the use to go to school instead of enjoying my life?

Sometimes you might feel very lonely in that relationship and decide to leave. Be careful not to jump in and out of relationships because you have created the situation by not knowing the best way to love your partner so that both of you can love and feel loved. When you jump in and out of relationships, remember, what are you teaching your children? Jumping in and out of relationships hardens the heart and you lose your credibility as a woman who values and respects herself.

Blended Family Relationships

Blended families are when a couple brings children from previous relation-ships to form one big family. As hard as it is to blend two families together, it can be just as hard to keep them apart. My dad had two sons when he met my mother. I only knew about this when I was 10 years old. My stepmother came to visit my brothers and she brought clothes for them and nothing for me. My one brother, Godfrey, who is late now, asked his mother, "Where are Rose's clothes?" She said that she had not brought anything for me. Godfrey was very upset and told her that she knew he had a sister and how come she did not bring anything for her? He then took some of his t-shirts and gave them to me. After that, he took my hand and we left her, going back to our house.

She tried to stop my brother, and I will never forget what my brother Godfrey said to her, "Mother you know very well that Rose is my sister and we live together in the same house. Mama (meaning my mom), treats me like her own. Why are you trying to break us apart?" With that, we left her, with her in disbelief.

My mother had never told me that Godfrey and Andrew were my stepbrothers. When I asked her that day after seeing this stepmom, she said that she did not see the use of dividing us. We had the same DNA so there was no point in her telling me that we had different mothers. To this day until now, most people never knew about this except my relatives only. I grew up very close with my brothers and we were inseparable. This only happens when you as the woman keep the children together.

Once you show a kid that you are not loved and are different, that alone kills the family unity. You can be married to a man with, or without children. How are you going to blend the families? It's a team effort between you and the spouse, to keep the family together, no matter who brought kids into the marriage.

It's your responsibility to be there for your children. Don't lose your focus when this guy gives you all the attention that you had missed since the passing of your husband that you forget about your children. Don't be that widow that ends up forgetting about her children and runs away with this Mr Nice guy. Find out if he embraces your children like his own and vice versa. Its common sense, that you also accept his children like your own, if you expect the same from him.

The question I'm sure that comes to your head is who is going to be the disciplinarian in this blended family dynamic? Sometimes the children can turn these two parents against each other, especially if the kids do not like the new partner that has come into their lives, through their parents. Now it means both of you must be on the same page with the discipline, when it's a no, it's the same from both parties not different from one parent to the other. This creates friction and biases in the relationships. Making the house rules and making sure that they are implemented must be teamwork too. If you were an impatient person then you must learn to be very patient as both families try to find each other in this new dynamic.

Kids need reassurance that your relationship with them is not going to be affected with this blended family situation. It is recommended to continue to have that quality time with the children you had before the other family came into their lives. This should also continue with your partner and his children.

There should also be times when the family swap parents and go for bonding times with his children and he goes with your children too. That way it keeps the relationships with both parent's fluid and no biases. Most of the times when two families come together, they outgrow the previous housing situation. Discussions which include the children should be held as to who will move and who will share space.

Take into consideration the age of the children when deciding to move them across town. Who is in high school, middle school and other extra curriculum activities that can get disrupted with the move? If this situation is relevant to you then it's wise to postpone the move until its ideal for everyone. I have seen children that really got disrupted with these moves and some will be traumatized for a while. As parents, you need to be mindful of things like this.

Don't forget to go through your final emotional detox, before you get remarried, so that you do not carry the dust particles from your previous baggage into the new relationship. Remember you have a choice to not get into it if you are not comfortable with it.

Love is felt and not spoken

"A real man can't stand seeing his woman hurt. He is careful with his decisions and actions, so he never has to be responsible for her pain."
Unknown Author

Getting into new romantic relationships can be tough for anyone including widows and divorcees. When I came to Canada I fell in love with this man from my country. He seemed well put together and I thought I had found myself a good man. We were together for 2 years before my kids joined us from Zimbabwe. I had not seen my children for almost 6 years. It was lovey-dovey before my kids arrived from Zimbabwe, but that became history when my children arrived.

This guy started complaining that I was not spending enough time with him. I tried to explain to him to give me time so I can bond with my children since we had been separated for so long. I tried to get him to bond with the children and they were always fighting. One time I asked him to pick the kids up from school. When he came home with the kids, he said that my children were rude to him. The only thing he said was the kids need to know that he was going to be their dad soon and they needed to call him dad. My children were 21, 17 and 13 years old. I asked him to give them time so they can get used to the fact that I had a new man in my life. I told him that asking them to call him dad just like that was pushing them too far. I felt that it was up to the kids to call him what they felt comfortable with, but not by his first name of course. They were calling him Uncle, nicknamed him, "UNKERS". I thought it was ok because we were not married yet. The kids knew about him and me before they came to Canada. I thought things would get better with time, but they did not.

It came to a point where the relationship with him and my kids got worse. They were fighting all the time when he was around. At one time it was snowing, and I was at work. I asked him to pick up the kids up from school and he did not bother to go. Afterward, the children called me and told me that they had walked home because "UNKERS," did not come to pick them up. When I asked him about this, he denied their claims. He said that he went to school and could not find them.

To make matters worse he did not even bother to tell me that he could not find the kids. This went on for a while. He would tell me all these crazy stories of what the children had said and done to him. Every time, I tried to talk to the kids about it when he was around, he would storm out saying that I should trust him, enough to believe him. He said that I should not be verifying his stories against what the children were telling me. I was caught in between, and we started fighting about this as well.

I would ask him to sit down so we could resolve this with the children together. He would refuse or the children would be unwilling to sit down with him saying it was pointless as he did not like them. When he was around, the children started to avoid him, and it got to a point where he asked me which side I was on.

This situation had to come to a stop. I was the only person who had to put this situation to a stop. I told him I was finished with him and I did not want to see him again. It's funny, that after all this stress, he then tried to apologize for being selfish and not considering that the children also needed time with me. He added that he thought if he had lied about the children being disrespectful, he would get more attention from me. I thought, wow man! Who does that?

This man had lied to me on several occasions about what his ex-wife had done to him and what my children had done to him as well. Later I found out that he did not have a good relationship with his own children. He always spoke about how his ex-wife had turned his children against him. His children were living in the same city as him, but they never visited him that often. They spoke on the phone here and there.

That was a red flag that I did not see. I was subjected to emotional and psychological abuse. I was manipulated into doubting the trust and the love I had for my children. I was working as a domestic violence counselor. When it happens to you, you always think you can fix things. I tried to use my social work skills to calm things down every time, but it was a temporary fix.

Telling you this will make you see that things like this can happen to anyone. When you are the one who has the kids that are around a man who has no access to his own children, for reasons known to him, this can happen. What a mess! I felt I had let my children down! I should have seen the red flags, but I had been blinded by love.

This guy was the type of man who would tell you all the sweet nothings that every woman wanted to hear. I thought I had found myself a Mr. Right. I was wrong. This was a failed relationship. I had to choose my children and let that man, go. The relationship was getting toxic and it needed to end. I had to get a Peace Order to make sure that he does not come anywhere close to me and my children.

As mothers, we must love and protect our children from situations like these. As parents, we need to spend more time with our children, so we get to know them well. Had I believed all the lies this guy was telling me about my children, I would have lost my children because of his lies. I had to repair the relationship between my children and myself. I did not want my children to feel like I was going to abandon them if another man came along. I wanted them to know that I was not going anywhere, and I was not going to have some man or love to separate us, by planting some crazy ideas into my head.

For a while, I was kind of lost, with the loss of this relationship and was wondering that with my late husband none of this would have happened. That's life, it's never straightforward, and you must figure things out as you go.

It was a relief when my mother came to Canada in 2009. No matter how old you are, a hug from your mama always grounds you, makes you feel that you matter, and you are loved. She was a huge help for me to look after the kids as I worked my two jobs and sent myself through University. With my mother at home all the time, it gave my children backup moral support when I was at work or doing my school assignments. Things were going smoothly, and everyone was happy again.

In 2014, I thought I was ready to find love again and I met this guy from the Caribbean. He was widowed, so I thought we would have something in common as he was widowed too. He had been alone for the longest while which was a red flag, but I missed it. He told me he was ready for a long-term relationship and this identified with me too. I was looking for someone to settle down with. I was ready to get married if I found the right man, of course.

As soon as this man knew that he had won my heart things changed. One day he told me that he had a surprise for me. I got all excited, only to find out that he had built a house back in the Caribbean and he wanted us to move there. I thought to myself, dude, I cannot just get up and leave! I had my mother and my children here in Canada. Leaving the country was not an option. He said he had enough money saved for us to live a good life over there. I was stunned. He did not even consider whether I liked it there or not, I had a career here and I had no idea what I was going to do when I got to the Caribbean.

My mother was still alive then, and she had told me that she did not think he was a good fit for me. But I thought he would change. Now I believe that when your mother has a bad or negative vibe about a guy you are seeing, believe her. I call it, "**Intuition of the womb.**" The bond we have with our mothers is very strong and they can feel things that we cannot feel or see. Now I believe in this saying by Oprah Winfrey,

"When a man shows you who he is the first time, believe him because that's who he really is."

Breaking up with this guy was the best decision ever and I felt liberated. It was like a heavy weight had been taken off my shoulders. He did not have any issues with my children though. He loved my kids, but he was just so insecure that I would leave him first. That then turned him into a control freak. I thought he would loosen up. I had tried to work on this relationship because I was scared about what people would say when they heard that Rose, had another failed relationship!

Soon, I learned that *"You can never change a man until he is ready to change himself for the woman he loves, not a woman changing a man for her. I soon also learned that the only time when a woman can change a man is when he is a baby when the mother changes his diaper."*

14

MEETING MEN AGAIN

After these relationships, I decided to learn more about relationships and what makes them last. Now I am a certified international relationship and dating expert. I have done a lot of research about relationships and dating. I had gotten tired of making mistakes and missing the red flags when they popped up. This made me want to teach other people, such as widows or any individual to be true to themselves and not to remain in relationships that were not working for the sake of having a man or a woman in their lives.

A weekend in Pigeon Lake for women's retreat helped me to go on a proper healing journey. I found out there were a lot of things I was taking for granted. Those things included taking care of ME. I had placed myself on the sidewalk for the longest time. I was taking care of everyone's problems and forgot that I had a heart and emotions that needed healing desperately. I took it upon myself to change my life, by putting myself first, loving and adoring myself. I realized that no one was going to come and do this for me. It was my responsibility to take care of me, myself and I. Loving yourself will bring the best out of you.

I am a positive person and will continue to heal and help others to heal their wounds as well. I had to check the people I was spending time with. What was I learning from these people? Were they making me grow or making me doubt myself from the failed relationships I had survived? Were they holding the failed relationships against me and continuing to remind me about them or not? Some of my friends kept holding that against me. They would pass comments like, "It's funny that you seem all put together, but you can't seem to get a man. How many times are you going to try before you get it right?" I'm sure you may have heard these comments from your circle too.

I had used my pain to turn my life around and show other women that it can be done, and life does not have to end that way.

In some eyes, *I am still that woman who had failed relationships. What they don't realize is that I learned from that experience and used that experience to change my life and the life of others.*

Don't allow the opinion of others to change your future. No one has the key to your future except God. So never be in a relationship that you feel obligated to be in. Never love someone under duress, it's not good for your mental health and those around you especially your children.

The lesson here is that, in the two relationships, both men had relationship issues with their children. So instead of me seeing that as a red flag, I felt sorry for them. Why? because I had been separated from my children for 6 years. I felt for anyone who does not have contact with their children. I also thought I could change them to be good parents and good lovers. I soon discovered the hard way that you can never change a man until he is ready to do it himself. I missed all the red flags when I felt I was being controlled. I brushed it off thinking it will pass. It will never pass.

Remember, "**When a man shows you who he is the first time believe him because that's who he is.**" (Oprah Winfrey).

Go through the healing process and don't take short cuts. Never assume you are healed, which is what I did, because it will catch up with you. Those wounds will affect the romantic decision you will make for yourself in the future. You will feel sorry for people and you'll fall in love for the wrong reasons.

I hope those analogies did not scare the skirts out of you. This is the reality and it's happening every day. The good thing is, you can do something to stop is continuing, and start a happier life again.

Type of Guys You Will Meet in The Dating World.

There are so many men out there and it's hard to start going back on the market and choosing men once again. This can be fun too if you look on the brighter side.

Look at the bigger picture. Ask yourself to look at this guy across the table, if he lost his looks would you still be attracted to him? I am sure that men ask themselves the same question too, about the women they end up getting married to. Is it the physical looks or the heart of the man that is going to attract you to him? What is the age difference? Are you attracted to older or younger men?

I heard one woman saying that she felt sorry for those women that must start again after their first relationship is over. The first marriage they probably married to their high school sweetheart, but now they are getting married to an old man and are going to be bound in the home looking after these old men, as women outlive men. I thought to myself this could be true. So, be mindful of that, what you are comfortable with? I can't really tell you who to marry. It's your choice, what makes you happy?

When you start dating you will face some challenges, and this is normal. You will meet all sorts of men with different characteristics, attributes, different height, weight, and all shapes and sizes and from all walks of life. Who you will choose to spend the rest of your life with is totally up to you. Don't forget that those choices will affect your children as well. That's why the children need to be bound to help with the final assessment as to who will be their stepdad.

Now that you are single, nice and handsome men will start to catch your attention. You will ask yourself, where were all these men before? This is because when you are in a long-term relationship and all is well, you get blinded by love. You did not notice and have no reason to notice these handsome dudes. Now you are on the market and you're open and searching for that special man.

Here is the list:

Men from Other Races

- You will meet men from other cultures and races. Men with all different colors, shapes, sizes, different languages and accents from yours.

The One from Work

- Some people will call these guy friends, "work husbands." The purpose of these relationships would be to look out for you when you are at work. Someone you can pick on when you have a bad day, someone you can vent with and a shoulder to cry on.
- Before people know what's going on with the two of you, they will start to gossip about you having a boyfriend at work! Sometimes it's possible that you can have a boyfriend at the office. The only risk is you getting fired for being caught in the storage room with your man!
- Life can also get messy!

The One You Met Once but Still Send Messages

- This is the guy that you met on the bus, or at a party, or perhaps on the plane. These are the men that you meet once, exchange phone, but never really get time to date. Sometimes you can hang out here and there. This one will usually end up in the friend zone.

The Guy You Have A Crush On

- You admit having a crush on him and he will tell you that he is married, gay or he is not interested. Ouch!! You just shared your feelings and they have not been reciprocated. He thinks it's weird that a woman tells him that she has the hoots for him. When this happens, don't take it personally, move onto the next one. Crying over your bruised heart will not change this guy's mind. Ouch!

He Seemed Great Online

- You read his profile online and you were blown off by what he seemed to be. You shared the same interests. You were like two peas in a pod. You met him in person, and he is totally the opposite. You get disappointed again. But that's life in the dating world. Keep trying.

You Friend-Zoned Him There and Then

- It was love at first sight for him. You also thought he was a nice guy, but just as a friend only. He tries to take you out on a date, but you are not into him romantically. He understands, but he does not give up on you, he still tries his luck. Well, you tell yourself; I can keep him for emergencies, or you never know it might work after all. "Don't burn all your bridges." You tell yourself.

The Player/The Emotionally Unavailable/Busy Guy

- He is the guy that seems not interested in dating. He seems very busy. He is Mr Charisma; he has lots of connections and lots of friends. He is the party guy and loves attention. He calls you last minute for a date. He is always nowhere to be seen and always reappears when it's convenient for him. He is the type that will lead you on, and if you are desperate you will think he is the real deal, but that's who he is.
- If you are looking for something more serious you might want someone more consistent. I am sure are you getting too old for games, so to speak.

He Is Your Friend's Ex

- There is chemistry, but because you are not sure how your friend will react to this if you tell her about it. You like him, but you still turn him down, as your friend might not be too happy with you.

He Does Not Take "No" For An Answer

- He will not take **no** for an answer, no matter how much you tell him you are not a match. The more you say no, the more he will send you on a guilt trip for rejecting him. He is persistent to get under your skirt or maybe more but will not leave you alone. So, what are you going to do?

The One Night Stand

- Well, it was rosy the night before, in the morning it's like nothing happened last night. What's up with this guy?
- He promises to set up another date and all he does is, sex-text you. So much for the night, you guys hit it off.

The Emotionally Unavailable Man

- He is a casual dater. He is allergic to serious relationships and cannot date one person for too long. He has lots of trust issues and blames everyone for his dating problems, but himself. He needs to face his fears and deal with them. (more about this type of guy in the next chapter, Dating Smart).

He Just Vanished on You

- You thought he was a good match. You felt there was something going there. You shared some secrets and your heart has opened to him. You smile when you think about him. Suddenly, he is gone without any explanation and no forwarding contact information. You are confused. Was it your fault is it something you did? Is history repeating itself again? You have hurt once again.

Different Men & Personality Types

The different personality types in men are bad boys, seducers, artists, successful, the people pleasers and more.

The Bad Boy

- This is the type of man your mama will not approve of. She will have a heart attack when you bring him home to meet her. This personality type smokes anything that can get them high. They drink themselves stupid. They end up abusing their women too to show their buddies how tough they are. They end up in jail. These could be bikers; they dress tough with huge tattoos everywhere. For some reason this bad boy has a way with his charm, he will sweep you off your feet in seconds.
- Women are attracted to him like he is a magnet. Breathe and check your pulse. Is this what you want?

The Adventurer

- He is fearless. He tries all the scary things. He likes to try new things all the time. The issue is they have more than one woman at a time. It seems women accept this from this adventurous guy. You can never tame him; he is a wild horse and very controlling in relationships. They cheat on their women; this is a known factor, but women fall for this type of men like flies.

The Seducer

- This guy knows how to sweep you off your feet, he is the ladies' man. He only sees the world through his romantic perspective, this a magnetic to women. They pay full attention to women's needs. They are sexy and they know what to say to the women, exactly what they want to hear. Men look at them, as bizarre as they are a little too much. They can be very submissive until they get under your skirt and they vanish. They are repellent to long term relationships.

The Sexy Older Cradle Rocker

- He has lots of experience with women and he is emotionally stable. He is usually a woman's man. He is always on point with giving you special gifts and whisking you off to romantic dinners and vacations. He is very sophisticated; he is the type that will send a car to pick you up from work for a surprise vacation and will pay for everything including the clothes you will wear on the trip. He wears expensive clothes and cologne. You know the one that calls his name in the hallway!! Don't be surprised if he will give you a convertible for your birthday. He can afford it. Every woman would want this type of man especially if you are not interested in happy kids.
- He is tired of chasing toddlers all he needs is someone to keep him breathing and feeling good about himself. The only downside is he snores like a 16-wheeler truck. So, make sure you prop up his pillows so you can get a good night's sleep. Another thing to bear in mind is the need for you to offer to pay for small stuff so he does not think that you are a gold digger.

Successful Guy

- He is the dream guy for most women. He is financially stable and will give you the Hollywood lifestyle you have dreamt of. You are taken to fancy dinners, bought expensive gifts. He drives the latest model of the most expensive sports car, his house is stupendous, and he has a Rolex on his wrist.
- The only issue he might be away on a lot because of business trips. Dig deeper to see if he does not have any other life with another woman

elsewhere during his business trips. It's time to set your guy to work on this one. The choice is yours.

The Controller

- He is like your dad. Very controlling and will treat you like a little girl who cannot think for herself. Some women love this. Do you? Most of these guys date much younger girls that they control.
- He might be a good provider, but everything is done his way and his way only. He can be very obsessed with your moves and thinks you are cheating on him.

The Regular Guy

- He is very down to earth. Your mother would give you her blessing to marry this guy. He has stability and is interested in a long-term relationship that will end up in marriage. He will be there for you when you need him. He knows how to do housework and can help with cooking very nice meals. He can change a baby diaper with no problems, he is a family guy.
- The woman is the one that ends up in control of the relationship. He gets kind of boring as time goes by, as he is used to routines.

Women Pleaser Guy

- This is the best of them all. He is very loyal to his woman. He never raises his voice at his queen. Dominant women love this kind of man. He is like a little puppy following his owner around the house.
- The only thing is, every woman also loves a man who has some masculinity in him. I would want a guy who can protect me in times of trouble. This guy is very timid and very shy.

The Mama's Boy

- He is a very good man. He will treat you like a queen. He was taught from a young age to respect women, so you are safe he will not disrespect. Make sure you go to his house, so you can see if his mama's clothes are not in his closet. He might still be in his mother's basement.
- The only issue is, he loves his mother, and everything must go through his mama. You must be good to mama for you to date and get married to mama's boy. He is very datable, but he needs love and a lot of attention. He a very emotional guy who cries very easily, but he is very loving and caring. If you get married to this guy you have no issues with baby sitters as mama is there in a blink of an eye.

The Personalities You Should Avoid

The Overbearing or Dictator

This man wants you to be under his thumb. He will tell you what to wear, not in a loving way, but by giving you ultimatums. He goes like, "wear that or you are not going anywhere with me." I would prefer to be told, "you know babe, that red dress makes you look hot and sexy, please put in on tonight and those black heels, my, my, they elongate your legs," and vice versa. This type of guy is very insecure, jealous, and passive. He is always suspicious of your friendships with other men in your life than him. He is the one that will keep track of all your movements and wants to know most of the details of your daily events to the hour.

You will feel suffocated in a relationship like this. He will treat you like a kid who needs to be checked upon. He is overly protective and sometimes he feels you cannot think for yourself, as he tries to control all the decisions that you try to make for yourself. The choice is yours; you have the right to choose what relationship works for you.

The Emotionally Unavailable Guy

This is the guy that never shares with you and is never vulnerable around you. He will keep you at arm's length and never shows you some compassion too when you need it. He always has his walls up; it feels cold when you are around him. This is a very bad feeling as you should have some warm feelings when you are around your man. You will never be able to share his life fully as he is never going to open to you and he will not be able to let you be vulnerable with him, too. It seems like he is all closed off.

The Guy Who Keeps You as His Option

He makes his booty calls to you always after midnight. He will appear when his steady girlfriend is mad and not giving him what he wants (sex). He will call you, pretend to be really upset and needs you to comfort him. He will tell you all the nice things you want to hear from your man. He gets into your knickers and boom he is gone again. He will not even stay for breakfast. He will leave and will not call you to talk about what was bugging him when he showed up at your doorstep at 2.00 am.

It's clear you're his option when he is bored and when he has nothing to do. A man who loves you and respects you will not show up at your house or call you to come to his place after 12.00 am to hang out. Girlfriend, this guy wants to use you for sex and nothing else. You are better than that and you deserve to be respected and loved.

The Whatever Lazy Guy

This is the guy that will not put any effort into the relationship at all. He expects you to call him, set up all the dates and look for the meeting places. You will do all the giving and you will be getting zero in return. When you are dating someone, both of you should put in the work to keep the relationship going. If it's only you who must keep pouring into the relationship, then it's time for you to move on to someone who will appreciate you. This is not a healthy relationship as you will suffer from dating burn out, because it's going to suck all the energy out of you. Well, it's time for you to move your time and love to someone who will appreciate it enough to meet you all the way. Most of these guys are couch potatoes, as they enjoy watching TV and never really go out to socialize or network with other people outside their space.

The Male Chauvinist

This is the type of guy who has an over-inflated ego. He thinks only about himself and everything is all about him. He has no regard for other people's feelings let alone yours. It's like you must fit into his world, not the other way around. He is selfish and arrogant. This is the type of guy who treats women as second-class citizens. He is also the type of guy who belittles women and other people who do not belong in his class. He thinks women are weak and are objects for possession. His misplaced ego will make you try to prove him wrong and you will find yourself sucked into his negative energy.

When you find out that your guy is a chauvinist, it's time to run for the hills and get the man you deserve. I know some of the women grew up in this environment or culture where the man runs the women's lives. I think those days have sailed away. I stand to be corrected.

Pathological Liar

This is an individual that lies for no personal gain. He just lies through his teeth. He is very unreliable because you never know when he is telling the truth about anything. It's draining to deal with a person of this nature as he will make promises that he cannot keep. You can really trust him with his own life. For a relationship to thrive there must be trust and with this individual, trust me it will never happen. Can you imagine being with a person that you can never trust at all? He always has reasons why he cannot meet you for a date, why you cannot come to his house, or meet his family.

15

ARE YOU DATING MATERIAL YET?

"I believe that a lot of how people look is to do with how you feel about yourself and your life.

Happiness is the greatest beauty secret."

Tina Turner.

Look at what Tina Turner went through, to be where she is today. You can see that nothing is impossible once you put your mind to it. She did not dwell on her past but used the little strength she had to start afresh.

The first step is to make sure that you are at peace with the past. You have accepted that you a single woman now and it's now time to move on. Looking back is not going to change anything from your past. Ask yourself, "Are you .... ready to date again and find the love of your life?" If you are ready let's go to the next step.

Pray to God to get clarity about what else you need to do. Pray so you can get the strength and the help you need on this new journey.

God is faithful, he will lead your path, but you need to ask him for help and have faith that it will happen.

Getting back into the dating world can be a scary thing. The thought of getting involved with another man again, can stir up some scary emotions and induce anxiety. Make sure you go through the dating detox and just work on yourself and self-assess your readiness to dating.

Look at what you and I have gone through already! The beautiful thing is, we are still standing, and you are reading this book because you are alive and kicking! What can pull you down now that you have not experienced? What did not kill you before, now made you stronger than before! You and I went through the rollercoaster of life, but we are still here alive. We are like palm trees, my dear. As the hurricanes of life tried to blow us out, we stood our ground and just went with the flow of the wind. Now that the hurricane is over our roots have become stronger and deeper into the grounds of our hearts. Sometimes you need to go through hell to find your paradise. Now we deserve to be happy!!

All the dust has settled, and you are in your own zone of life. Someone you might have heard of is knocking on your door. This person wants some company as she cannot stand her own company. This person is popularly known as, "**Loneliness.**" Most people start to feel it at this stage of the journey. They are back to reality and they realize no one is paying attention to their wallowing, grieving, tantrums. Loneliness usually comes uninvited and can stay with you if she is welcomed in your company. Maybe your spouse died after a long illness, it means you started grieving when your husband was still alive. Some couples usually discuss what should happen to the surviving spouse in terms of remarrying and being happy after they have gone. You might say, "What if it was a sudden death?" Then sit down and have a conversation with yourself and your spouse in your head. I'm sure there was a time when this topic was mentioned in passing during your time together. It's a tough decision to make but must be made otherwise life will go on with or without you.

Letting go of the **victim mentality** will propel your healing five times faster than holding onto that wounded mindset. That victim mindset and limiting beliefs will continue to permeate everyone you talk to. Now that you want to move on to find love, stop walking around with your head down. You will only project yourself as a needy, clingy person with very low self-esteem. This will obviously chase the potential guys away. Playing the victim will also turn you into a more co-dependent individual who will need validation and pity from other people. When you shake off that victim mentality, you will get your power back as a woman of value, and your self-confidence will be raised. If you still cannot shake this mentality off, then start to re-evaluate why you cannot shake it off. Get yourself some professional help from a coach or a therapist.

Going into the dating world again is a new chapter in your life. What attitude to life have you developed since you have been on this widowhood or divorcee journey? Are you still looking at life with a **sulky attitude**? Holding onto that pain due to your loss will turn all that pain into bitterness and anger. I was bitter and angry too, but afterwards, I decided to let go, forgive and smile more. It helped me to dissolve the stress of life. Do you still wish to continue to live that life of woundedness, brokenness, poor me, pity party? You know living this life is like carrying a ton of bricks on your shoulders.

You deserve to be happy. The only person who is blocking that happiness is you and your mind. You still feel and think you **suck** at falling and finding love again? You probably failed because you were doing the same thing repeatedly expecting to get some amazing results from your outdated ways. This is your time to go after your dream life that you had shelved while you were taking care of the family and during the grieving period. There is nothing so insurmountable that can come between you and your happiness now besides YOU.

Remember that there is a time for everything; time to be born, time to die, time to grieve, time to heal and to move on. Don't continue to suffer in vain. After all, you still have the memories of your husband safely tucked away somewhere. Your late husband will remain part of your life no matter what, and whoever will come into life now will have to accept that. The ex-husband will still be in your life somehow, but you must move on and close that chapter.

Backlash

Before we go deep into this chapter, let's talk about the backlash that will be slapped into your face. You must be ready and know whether to respond to each one of them or walk away. Be warned that some of the critics are so bold that they can say things like these below to your face without any remorse: -

- "She had an affair while the husband was ill, that so pathetic."
- "She did not even love the husband anyway; everyone knew about it."
- "She only wanted insurance and pension benefits. Now she has gotten it, she will spend the money with her boyfriends."
- "The kids will miss their dad for sure. No one is going to be caring for them since she will be running away with her new lover. Those poor kids."
- "Oh, we knew that she was fake all this time. He was blinded by love, oh poor thing."
- They might give you those looks that you will feel like someone is stripping you naked with their eyes.

What you need to know is, you started off being this amazing caregiver looking after your ailing husband, to a heartless, good for nothing widow, because you have decided to move on and find love again. It's tough to think that some people will think like this. All the kind gestures and words they were giving you when your hubby passed on, will soon vanish. They will soon forget the trauma that you went through losing your better half.

People will not stop to have their own opinion of you, no matter what. You need to know that you can never please everyone, including yourself. You cannot control what people think or say about you, no matter how hard you try to please them. The only thing you can control is YOU, and how you will react is all up to you. That will then determine how you will move on, with your future.

You know, it's not everyone who is going to be against your moving on. There will be some open-minded people that will view this as a noble decision for your life. You can go back to the self-love part of this book. For you to be happy and have self-love or self-acceptance, you must do what makes you happy. Just be mindful that what you are doing is not going to blow up in your face later in your future dating life.

One thing you need to keep in mind is, those people talking ill about you, might have never been in your shoes, so they have no idea what you are going through right now. Your mind might start running some fears about what might go wrong with the new relationship that you have not even started yet. This is normal by the way; just remember what your goal is.

It's time for you to develop a thick skin and focus on YOU. Your life will not change unless you do something about it. I remember when I moved on, to find love, I was called names and was accused of being a gold digger for taking my late husband's money and then running away with the children. These naysayers are the same people that will jeer at you when you fail and call you a loser. At first, it tore me apart; I don't want to lie. I used to come home and cry in my bedroom. My children would know that if my bedroom door was closed, I was crying. My kids, Rue, Ronnie and Ropa, would come into my room and tell me that things would be okay. They would remind me that they loved me no matter what happened. I held onto that promise and it kept me strong during my grieving journey and when I decided to move on.

In-Laws or Outlaws

These will remain part of your life no matter how hard you try to wiggle out of it. You were married to their own so that makes you part of them. They will have opinions about your choices whether you like or not. In my case too, they had an opinion as to how I was supposed to live my life. I was told because their son had paid the bride price, which made me vulnerable to them controlling how I was to live my life. They will certainly feel like you are cheating on their son as well as betraying them. I guess it's normal for them to feel this way, they are humans too. Maybe the best way would be to let them know that you have decided to move on and find love. This is tough I know and am not sure how widows have the guts to do this. It feels like you are shooting yourself in the foot. They also need to understand that you have not forgotten about their son and that he will still be part of you. I think in this case it's easier when you have been divorced from their son. They will probably rejoice that you are moving on out of their lives. Make sure they understand that you will not cut off the relationship with their grandkids. It's their blood too. But if they are not interested in connecting with their grandkids, don't force it. With time they will reconnect again.

It's awkward in some cultures to bring along your new love to family events in which your in-laws are invited too. Some cultures welcome this so that it makes it easier to communicate with the children and yourself. Don't forget to ask God to give clarity on how to handle this. Time will come when you will be able to stand up for yourself and your children when you know how to love yourself.

"You will love and care for yourself because that's when the best comes out," (Tina Turner).

The moment you start falling in love with another man, it will feel like you are in love with two men at the same time. The thoughts of history repeating itself will rush back into your small brain. It's normal to have these feelings but you must decide whether you want these self-doubts to keep you stuck in your pain or not.

You might also be scared to be vulnerable to another man again. You know what? You will remain vulnerable to your fear and be miserable and lonely for the rest of your life. You will never know what will happen to your love life until you try again. Don't let the fear of the widowhood experience, steer you away from finding someone to love and care for you.

One thing to bear in mind is that widowhood has prepared you for marriage. You can put this on your resume for finding love (your on-line profile.) That makes you a catch. At least you have been there, you are dependable, and you know it feels. You have learned to navigate through the chaos that comes along with relationships.

Remind yourself of this saying,

"You will never know how strong you are until being strong is the only option." Bob Marley.

A Salvation Army Officer (Pastor), Major Mabhiza was my Pastor when my husband passed on. Mrs Major Mabhiza had also lost her husband a few years earlier, and she said to me, "Rose you need to have an elephant skin to survive as a widow. You need to focus on your life and do what's best for you and your children." I learned to focus on the present, the now, which was where my happiness was. When I came to Canada, most people in my community knew I was widowed when I dated that guy from my country. They still talked bad about me even though some of them knew what a jerk this guy was. After I broke up with him, that's when I found out that some people in my circle knew about his deviant behaviors, but they never had the guts to tell me about it.

This will also happen to you. So, never rely on other people to find out the truth about the man you are dating. You must do the work yourself. Talk to his relatives, friends and other family members as well as his workmates if you can. If you rely on what he tells you, he might lie about his life like what that guy did to me. I am not scaring you, but you must be sure who you are getting involved with. If he is dilly-dallying about you talking to his family or friends, then that's a red flag. You need to ask him what he is hiding from you.

It's time for you to know more about who you are and to have a deeper level of self-love. For this to happen you must develop your self-awareness.

Self-Awareness

This is the power of knowing yourself. It is having radical honesty with yourself. You must know your strengths and weakness, habits, desires, and triggers. Having **Self Awareness** will help you to transform any area of your life. People without self-awareness will remain stuck in their blame-shifting mindset.

Look in the mirror, what do you see? Do you love what you see? Or you cannot stand that image of you staring back at you? Self-awareness is the ability to see yourself clearly, how you fit into the world and how others see you. This allows you to take your power back which was stolen from you during the trauma of your loss. This makes us stronger and creates stronger relationships, we become more loveable and have the strength to love again.

How to Know if You Have Self-Awareness?

- You are more fulfilled and are a good communicator
- You are less likely to lie or cheat in the relationship
- You are more creative with your life
- You are not clingy and needy
- You independent and have high self-confidence.

If you have self-awareness, when things go wrong your brain will not go to asking why it happened. Asking why will spiral negativity into your mind. Instead, you should ask yourself, what you can do to improve the situation. Asking why leads us away from the real issue. It sends us further into the victim mentality. Approaching the problem with the, "what can I do?" to improve the situation will give you more alternatives to change the situation. Asking why persistently, clouds our minds and perception of life. When you say, "oh why me," you go into this victim mode, but if you say, "what can I do?" you are empowering yourself, to find a solution.

- What can you do to heal?
- What can you do to find love?
- What can you do to change your outlook?

How does this statement sound to you, "**Why** can I do, to find the solution?" awkward right? In order to find the zeal to defeat the naysayers, you need to learn from some widows who have gone full circle. Those women who were once widows and have found love again. Talk to them, to get some

177

insight into what to expect and how to deal with it. It makes me happy to see women who have made it in finding love again and are happily married again.

Your children

Your children come first in every decision you make that will affect their well-being. Don't sacrifice their welfare and security because you have found your dream guy. Does this guy embrace your children like his own? Take some time to sit down with them so they can understand that you need to love and to be loved too. Most of the times the children want to feel secure in this love triangle so that they feel that they will remain in your life and you in theirs. They want to make sure that this new man is not replacing their dad and that you are not forgetting their father completely too. They might give you that look like you have two heads, or you are out of your mind, especially when the children are still young below their teenage years. This might make you question your decision to find love. This is the reason that you need to make them understand that their father will still hold his golden place in both your lives.

Reassure them of your continued love and presence in their lives. When they ask questions don't be defensive and confrontational with them. Forcing them to accept the new guy will end up in creating tension between you and the children. Once the children understand that you are human just like everyone else, they will want what makes you happy. You just must trust God and he will help your children to be on the same page with you.

Branding yourself ready for dating

Now that you have chosen to get back into the dating pool, you need to brand yourself. This means you must recreate a new version of you. The old self no longer exists, as you have changed since the funeral. When you look at yourself in the mirror, I'm sure you can see that you have lost that spark that you used to have. This spark needs to be rekindled so you can be ready to walk into the dating world full of confidence and self-worth.

This branding of yourself is like in business. You need to find and create that special quality about yourself that you did not know existed. Something that will make you stand out and special in the crowd among other singles out there. Look at yourself and identify what is your strongest feature. Is it the smile, legs, eyes, hair, body shape a whole, your butt, boobs, your height, etc. Then build your brand around those feature(s).

Ask yourself why would someone new want to date you now? This will help you to build your brand and your confidence. Another area to think about is your attributes. What are your strengths, which will make you unique?

Remind Yourself That You Are A Catch

Reminding yourself that you are a catch will keep you in your feminine energy. You must love you and respect yourself before someone else loves you. When you are comfortable in accepting the beautiful you, then you can exude an air of fabulousness. When you can carry yourself with pride, then men will want to date you. Think and speak highly of yourself, not boasting, of course, it's very attractive to men. Men are attracted to women who are pleasant and exciting to be round. Stop self-bashing its very unattractive.

Your "I Love Me" List

You are a catch because:

- I am smart and intelligent and one of a kind.
- I am sweet and funny
- I am intellectually stimulating
- I very happy with myself
- I am warm.
- What makes me unique and loveable?
- What am I bringing to the relationship?

- Do I feel sexy at all?
- Do I practice self-care and self-love?
- Do I feel proud of myself?
- Do I celebrate my accomplishments?
- Am I approachable?

If you keep these in check you will be so captivating that man who will want to date you!

16

TO BE SAVVY, EMPOWERED AND CONFIDENT

I am sure you don't want to go into a relationship and end up unhappy or become a doormat. What you need to think about is, the things that matter in love, are not necessarily the things that matter even if you have a good job or a beautiful body.

• Don't attempt to change the guy:

Don't treat or think of men as objects. Trying to change them, fix, save and domesticate them might destroy their ego. They are their own persons. A man will change when he is ready. He will change for a woman he loves, not the other way around. It's not up to you to try and steer him on the life road of your choosing, it's up to him. Forcing this will cause you heartburn and might snatch away a lot of your baby-making years or destroy many years of companionship and love. You must show him that you are the prize in this thing. You will do this by maintaining your self-worth, self-love, self-value and self-acceptance.

• Be the queen bee of the hive:

Be in your feminine energy so you can have the men to be the worker bees, giving, doing, nurturing and offering the love to you. Men love to buzz around you doing what they can to please you. Be appreciative of the things they do to steal your heart. All it means is, if you are the one putting in all the work in the relationship, then men will lean back and get bored.

Remain a mystery to them. Men are hunters they love to hunt and when they catch the prey, they will appreciate it more.

Once you change this dynamic, then they will shift their focus, they will take you for granted and will start to do things that please him and not you. He will start to do things at his own pace, like when to call you back or text you. Does that sound familiar?

• Don't be afraid to be vulnerable:

Since you have had your feathers ruffled the other way, you have survived the roller coaster life, and it's time to tame your mane. You need to turn into a teddy bear that he can run to, to cuddle up with. The **she-ego** needs to be put into the back seat of your car. He needs to feel like you are a haven for him to reveal his vulnerability. Stop nagging him about his silly behaviors and why he does certain things a certain way. Show him you can also be vulnerable around him and he will know you are a human being, who is ready for a relationship too.

• Show that you care:

Let him be that little boy around you. Men are usually not comfortable with doing this. When he knows he can trust you, he will be able to let go of his guards. He will know you can hold his feelings safe.

• Be open about how you feel about things.

This will make him respect you. An independent, confident, smart and sassy woman will express her feelings freely. If you are nervous on the first date, then let him know that you are shaking inside like a leaf and he will understand. If you had a bad day at work express it. If he listens to you then he is interested in you. If you are upset with his behavior, then let him know in a loving and feminine way. Don't treat him like he is your child or reprimand him like he is back in kindergarten. If you are interested in him then show your interest, but don't chase him. Don't mother him, you will seem to be very controlling and smothering him. Just dive into your goddess world of soft, sensual, tender, tear-lined, funny and playful self.

- Date, for the right reasons:

You looked for reasons to stop grieving, dating might be among the significant ones. You want to experience life again since you have realized that grief was holding you back. The new guy is not your counselor or therapist, so don't put the weight on him to make you happy. It's too much to ask from him. So, don't try to make this innocent guy fill in the void in your life/heart. You want to love, then create a loving environment without hidden agendas.

- Be yourself:

Don't pretend to be someone you are not. Drop your walls so you can be your sweet self again. I know this can be challenging since your personality had to change to fit all these roles that came with widowhood. Don't overshare who you are on the first date. Especially the juicy stuff about your late husband or ex. It can drive him away.

- Get family approval on both sides

A smart sassy woman will not force her man to meet her family before he is ready for this. She will not force her way to meet his family before he is ready for that. But it should not be an excuse for not meeting the family after dating for more than six months. Both families need to be in approval of this new relationship and children can be the biggest culprits in destroying your new-found love, if they don't approve. So, play your cards right.

- Dating a widower:

Be very clear about the kind of relationship you are looking for. Widowers can date to get companionship and not a relationship so make it clear what you are looking for. This is because widowers always think that they have an issue with not being able to deal with loneliness, so they look for companionship. They can also be ready to date, but just make sure you know what you are getting yourself into, before investing too much of your time into this.

- Work on your insecurities:

You should stop yourself when that self-defeating voice creeps into your mind, telling you that you are not good enough. Don't kill the buzz by being very negative about yourself, your late husband or your ex. Don't be fixated on the previous sarcastic compliments given to you by your haters or naysayers that you cannot take compliments. A sassy and confident woman will be able to hold her head on her shoulders and be able to be the best that she can on this date and the ones to follow. You are the best version of yourself, remember that!

- Don't be paranoid:

Being paranoid about your past, that history might repeat itself is not an attractive habit or behavior. No one wants to feel like they are under surveillance from an FBI agent. So, keep your suspicions under control don't let them overtake you. Let the paranoia out when he has done something that really calls for your suspicions to run loose.

Keep it in check when he does something that reminds you of that immature idiot, weird, sneaky and control freak you once dated. Don't paint all men with one brush, there is some very good and decent man out there looking for a woman like you to spend the rest of their lives with.

Getting Your Groove Back

Now that you have healed your wounds, checked all your emotions and your mindset is reset. You are ready to start your journey into the dating world. There are things that you need to look at. I am sure by now your emotions are all stabilized and you continue to work on them. Remember the healing journey is a continuous process, this is because you will continue to meet things, situations, and people that will remind you of your late husband or your ex. You must keep up with your self-care and self-love.

You might choose to remain single, it's not a problem. Remember it's your choice to remain on your own. It is not fun when you end up single, because you did not do something about it, and you will be settling not choosing to be on your own. You might tell yourself, "I'm past my sell-by date." Says who? You are not a vegetable that has a shelf life! Remember, "age is just a number that you are not supposed to scrutinize every day!" I have seen some 95-year-olds getting married! I am yet to see a bill that prohibits marriage past a certain age. Whatever choice you end up taking, please do me a favor, have some fun doing it. Just don't settle when you can still make a choice.

How to Brand Yourself For The Dating World

You are your own creation and are unique in your own right. That's why you are called by your name. Be proud of yourself. You have made it this far and this is just the beginning of your next chapter.

This is the time when that fear planting voice coming from Mr Butterflies and his best buddy Mr Nervous will pay you an unexpected visit. These two buddies can sway you away from your chance to find love again. Acknowledge their presence and their visit and tell them to move on their journey as you want a new life without their help. You will find yourself finding your courage to find love again.

1. Find yourself first, how do you feel about yourself?
2. Your wardrobe does it depict how you feel or look?
3. Are you financially secure?

Finding yourself: - how do you feel about yourself?

For you to be ready to date and love someone, you must be emotionally ready for this.

Ask yourself, whether you feel ready to date?

Why do you feel you are ready for this chapter of your life?

Can you date yourself at this time?

What are you going to do differently from the last time you went on a date?

Don't expect new results and yet still do the same things you did years ago when you married your late husband or your ex. Times have changed and so have people. While you were in your marriage the world was changing and now you feel like a fish out of water in the dating game. This should not freak you out. You just need to reset your dating clock to start again.

Do you have a fear of being seen? I mean do you have issues with receiving compliments from people? Do you defect or change the topic when someone praises you for wearing a sexy outfit, nice perfume, or new hairstyle? Do you feel guilty at accepting these compliments? This is a crucial step in opening yourself up that you must overcome. If you cannot accept compliments it means you cannot receive love and give it in return. You have what I call, "Love Repellant Syndrome." You will need to practice accepting and giving compliments.

Do you have a fear of not being good enough? Don't allow these fears to overrule your chance to find and give love. When these insecurities flood your mind, they block the flow of positive energy that attracts love and abundance in your life. Accepting yourself, and the perceived flaws, you will open space in your heart and release all the blockages holding new love entering your heart. On the same note, stop placing judgments about others.

When you find yourself putting others down, or speaking ill of others, it not only lowers your love vibration, but it also closes off your heart from opening to love. It means you are creating negative energy around you which will send the same negative vibrations into the universe. Try to practice compassion, be gentle with yourself. When you judge others harshly, it means you will be quick to judge yourself too. Remember what you send out into the universe is what you will get back?

While I'm at it, how is your health? Do you get yourself checked out to make sure that everything is running smoothly? Your health is the backbone of everything. You need your health to function well physically, mentally, emotionally and psychologically. When you are healthy you will feel happier, and more productive at work than when your health is down the drain. I know when I am not feeling well, I feel like crap, I feel frustrated and very irritable.

Going into the dating pool, you need to be feeling good about yourself. Take time to be with yourself, pamper yourself and take yourself out for vacations. Go out to movies and dinners so you can just enjoy life on your own. That way when someone comes into your life, you know how to make yourself happy and you don't have to wait for the new guy to make you happy.

Learn to have **fun,** laugh at yourself and dance to music in your car, shower and your house like no one is watching. Find humor in your life again. When I'm in my car, I'm in my sanctuary. I listen to my old school music and I dance and sing along. I don't pay attention to the weird looks that I get from other drivers around me. They don't know me, so who cares? You need to focus on you, what makes you happy not **what will people say**. Don't resign your life to endless grieving and mourning. Remember widowhood is the destiny that you never opted for.

Eat healthy meals and drink lots of water. Add more vegetables to your plate. Cut down on sweets and fast foods, pop, and greasy foods. They are not good for your health. Make home-prepared meals for your lunch to work it's cheaper and healthy. Sometimes you must drink or eat even when you don't feel like it. Remember not to comfort eat. That's using food as a quick fix to your problems or issues in your life. Healthy eating is your passport to healthy skin and a great figure. You are what you eat. Be mindful of what you are putting in your mouth.

How many hours of sleep are good for you? A good night's sleep is the biggest beauty secret that you can give yourself. It is inexpensive, it's something you can teach yourself and you can keep track of what's best for you. Good sleep helps to rejuvenate your body, mind, and spirit. If you can't sleep well get professional advice from your physician.

Check your daily schedule. What are the kinds of people you are spending most of your time with? Are you learning anything from them? If they are sucking the life out of you, you need to delete them from your contacts. They are not worth your time. Remember you are on a mission to get yourself, "A MAN," of your dreams. You don't want to start this journey feeling like you are living in a borrowed body, mind and spirit.

Is your physical health on point? How much exercise do you get for your body to remain active? Take some time to stretch your muscles. An active body creates a good environment for a healthy brain. It also improves your sleep, your emotions as well your looks too. Nobody is too old to exercise, and you don't have to go to the gym to get some exercise. You can do some exercise in your home. Take a walk after work, run up and down the stairs

It's time to stop dreaming about feeling better and doing something about it. You need to get to a point where you are, "sick and tired of being sick and tired." When you get to this point then you will know you ready to get out of that dry spell and get into something new. Your next step is to set out some realistic goals so you can have something to work towards.

Your Wardrobe and Your Outlook

When I look great and sexy, I feel like a million bucks and walk with a spring in my step. I like to look good all the time. It makes me feel happy when I look my best. So, it does not matter what kind of body shape you have, you need to learn to dress it up accordingly. Since you have been through the wringer, with what you went through in the past, dressing up is the last thing on your mind. But, it's time to lose the sweat pants, the oversize housecoats and plug into the trendy fashion gal!

When some people start to tell you to change your wardrobe, you might get into your defense mode and probably say, "What's wrong with what I am wearing now?" Well, it depends on what you are wearing now. What we wear and the colors affect our moods. Research has confirmed this. Try this and you will see its true. Wearing dull colors makes my mood run low and I feel like there is no excitement in life. You don't have to buy expensive clothes from the big brand stores to look good.

Take yourself window shopping to see what's out there. This is the best way to see how you can dress differently for different occasions. This is the time you need to look sexy and trendy. When you go shopping try out some clothes and in most retail stores, they can show you how to dress your body shape accordingly. It also depends on what the best feature on your body is. You also need to learn how to walk in a straight line, breath in, boobs out and walk like you just won the world.

I have always loved to express my emotions, my feelings and my excitement for life through fashion. I love to look different from everyone else. I am very bold with colors; I can rock any color and I will feel comfortable in it. Fashion can be fun especially when you are transforming your life.

- Know Your Body Shape and Your Limitations

When you go into a store, ask the fashion stylist or consultants, they will walk you through what's good for your body shape.

You need to know which style makes you look sexy, and small or bigger in the right places. You should know the parts of your body that you are not comfortable with. Some women have big biceps and they try to hide it by wearing clothes with sleeve, short, or cap sleeves.

When it comes to pants. What's your body shape like? If you have a wider waistline, then the low rise will not work for you. Also, be careful that when you wear the low-rise pants as everyone around might just enjoy a free view of your undergarments? That's a no, no, for ladies who want to be classy and sexy. If you have a small waist, then wear the high-waisted pants, they keep your waist as the focus on your body. Know what's flattering for your body shape. I know, I have a small waist; I have issues with pants, I must get them altered sometimes. I am gifted with a big behind, so I make sure I wear clothes that accentuate that. What are you gifted with?

- What's Your Strongest Parts or Points of Your Body?
- Don't waste too much time scrutinizing your body shape. If you don't like any part, if you can do something about getting it fixed, then if money permits, do it. If not, find ways to hide it or deal with it. Being sexy is not about having a proportional body shape. It's about how you carry yourself. It boils down to being self-confident. Learn to play around with different styles of clothes so you can feel sexy and good about how you look. Draw attention to your best features, the ones you feel the most confident with.
- Show "One End at a Time."

If you are going on a date or a night out with the girls and you want to look sassy, make sure to dress up and be girly. If you are going to be wearing a mini skirt and high heels, make sure you don't look trashy in it. Pair it up with a nice blouse that does not show off too much cleavage otherwise you look like a cheap girl on the loose. Remember, you must look sassy, classy and sexy. Trashy is not sexy, it's cheap and a no, no. If it's a set with a short skirt or shorts and a blouse with a very low neckline then throw a chiffon scarf to cover up. Don't display it all, just pick one focal point at a time.

How to Look Expensive and Classy on A Shoe String Budget

1. Wear sunglasses when going into the sun. Look for what's the trend and buy the dopest.
2. Bold jewelry, like big pearls, big chokers, and small earrings.
3. Wear scarfs, they can add some classy style to your outfit. A Plain dress, pair it up with a floral scarf, look for trendy ways to wear the scarfs on You-tube.
4. Have some chic necklaces that go with a lot of your outfits.

5. Get some belts to add to your outfits, skirts, dresses or on top of some tops. There are reversible belts that save money.

6. Have some cute handbags. They add style to your outfit. Your purse or handbag should not look like an overnight bag especially when you are going on a date.

7. Dark blue jeans make you look chic, clean, slim and expensive.

8. Pointed shoes look chic and classy. I know the rounded toe is more comfortable, but sometimes they are not forgiving especially when you have big feet like mine.

9. Turtle neck to wear with blazers.

10. Have that black and red dress in your closet for the night outs.

11. If you can have your clothes tailored then that's even better, then you can have clothes for your specifications.

12. Don't wear clothes that are too clingy. Wear your size to look classy, not looking like you borrowed the clothes or the hand me downs.

13. When choosing shoes, the heels wear something comfortable, if you are wearing heels for a date carry a pair of flats in the car, just in case your feet get tired.

14. Have some off-shoulder dresses when you are going on a date, and pencil skirts. Remember that tucking in your blouse or shirt on one side at the waist will give you that chic look and highlight your waist. Have some fitted dress as well.

15. Don't leave your confidence at home when you leave the house every day. It will get you a long way.

16. Check your posture when you walk.

17. Never leave home without your fabulous smile, its answer to your nervousness.

Your Makeup

This can be a challenge for many. You can do the best you can instead of going around like a plain jack or a grade 9 schoolgirl. When you wear makeup, you will feel different and add some lipstick. Check your skin tone to see which color goes with your skin tone. After grieving, your skin needs a lot of work. You need to start taking care of it. Makeup also looks as good as the skin under it. It means cleansing, moisturizing and toning it to keep it hydrated. It does not have to be expensive or time-consuming, it just needs to be suitable for your skin tone. To top off your skincare, drink lots of water, eating lots of greens and wear sunscreen when you go in the sun.

Just don't pile your skin with a lot of layers trying to cover up your scars or age spots. Be kind to your skin. Don't forget the lipstick. Most men love lipstick especially red or pink. I love the violet or purple. It's so smooth and striking to catch his attention. Well if you don't like lipstick then put some lip gloss, to make your lips pop out.

Your Hair

You might need to look at your hairstyle. I know I had to do a total makeover for my hair. Look at the color, you might need to change the color add some highlights. If your hair is not up to date, your whole outfit will fall out of place. Don't always go around on your bad hair day, it's not advisable especially now when you are searching for the love of your life. First impressions always matter. Changing your style will give you that fresh start. You will need something that will make you cry with joy when you look at yourself in the mirror. Something drastic would be great. The best is to go to a hairstylist or check some magazines for different hairstyles. Make sure you choose something within your budget and manageable too.

When you go out, make sure your hair is down. That will give you a more relaxed look. The bun might look either scruffy or too serious. Your job is to create that spark, without him even being aware of it.

Let your light shine and make eye contact with the dude you might see to be appealing to you. I can't say this enough. It will send signals to him to pay some attention and tell him, "I find you interesting." But be gentle don't scare the skirts out of this guy.

Be Financially Secure

Are you financially secure? Going into a relationship and hoping to get your financial instability to be solved by this new guy is a huge risk to take. I have seen some women becoming co-dependent on the new guy. As a result, this guy becomes frustrated with the extra responsibility thrown at him. He retaliates and abuse becomes imminent. The woman will find herself trapped in this loveless relationship because she cannot support herself and her children. To avoid this, be financially independent. Some widows get remarried to men who will con them out of their spousal benefits. There are men that will marry these vulnerable widows just to get to their bank accounts. Once they get access to the money, they squander it and when the money is gone then the widow becomes a victim of abuse. So, widows out there be mindful who is falling for you. Are they genuinely in love with you or they are after your widowhood benefits?

First Impressions: Men Are Visual Creatures

First impressions are very important, in that this is what will stick in his mind when he thinks of you. This might also set the standard for your way out of the widowhood and divorcee loneliness storms, and into the sunshine again.

Gregg Michaelsen said, "***Men are animals and we are visual. When we choose a woman, we do go for things like values and all the other stuff, but when it comes to first impressions......***

well, it is what it is."

For you to **be seen** make yourself available, don't hide under a pile of baggy clothes, when you can wear something sexy. Put yourself in the view of men. This can be a big challenge if you have been on a dry spell for a while. It feels awkward at first, I know. So instead of getting your food from the drive-through window in your car, park your car and walk inside. Sit down for a while and just look around while you are waiting for your order. Take your sexy time to pick up your order and get the condiments and the cutlery. If you see someone attractive there, make eye contact and just smile for some seconds. This will show them that you are approachable. Another tip, when out in the public stop frowning for nothing, it scares the good guys away. Being approachable is key in dating.

Continue to believe you are **a catch** and you will feel like a catch. The other thing also that usually destroys women's confidence is their self-talk! What are you telling yourself when you look in the mirror? Continue to tell yourself "I am beautiful, hot and sexy." until you believe it, it does not matter your colour, shape and your height. I know that the stress and the pain of widowhood might be triggered once you start dating. Remember not to let this sway you away from being the best you can. Turn this around and start telling yourself, you can do this, "I am a very attractive woman."

When you go on dates you should wear something comfortable. Don't worry about wearing that expensive designer dress on the first date but look classy and beautiful. Men are blind sometimes; they might not even notice that you are wearing a designer dress. So, don't go out of your way and spend money on an expensive outfit for that first date. You are not getting engaged or meeting his family members yet! Just don't dress like you are going on a field trip with Mother Theresa!

Check your emotions as you go out. Men can sniff out bad energy and bitterness. Make sure to dump the insecurities, jilted spirit and the not good enough labels in the garbage can. Men have insecurities of their own too. Most of them fear rejection with a passion. They might try to make it seem like they are disinterested in you. For this reason, you need to make sure that you don't lose your cool and try to show him what you are made of. The mean girl in you might start mouthing off your anger, just keep your composure. This indicates that you are prone to attaching to his, "negative meanings" this behavior makes it easy for you to fall into the victim role. Therefore, it is very important for you to have your emotions in check so you can withstand situations like this.

So be the better woman and not succumb to these powerless actions. Checking your emotions will also help you to defeat any self-sabotaging thoughts and behaviors that will not serve your purpose. Show your date that you are a high-value woman, with set boundaries. Give yourself time to change into the woman you wish to become. Push through the fear, the insecurities and ignore the mean girl inside your head who is always telling you that you are not good enough, smart enough, pretty enough, feminine enough, young enough and outgoing enough. Excessive emotions do not work with men. Your emotions can control your actions and that is not great when it comes to men. Excessive emotions can also lead you to feel sorry for men that are abusive as you might start feeling sorry for them, instead of being realistic with them.

How to Catch His Attention In A Crowd

Here are tips on how to show that you are single, searching and available to date. These have worked for a lot of women and you can see which ones you are more comfortable with. I know some of you are now thinking that I am giving these tips to be hookers and pick up men in bars for a one-night stand. These tips have worked for some women that have met their husbands. What you find depends on what you are looking for: -

- Use the five-second rule, look at the guy, lock your eyes with his and look away. Don't stare at the guy this will freak him out.
- Look at the guy and toss your hair to the side and look back again at him and smile broadly.
- Brush up against him accidentally just to catch his attention.
- Nodding your head at the man you seem to be interested in and pointing to an empty chair inviting him to sit down. If he is interested in you too, he will come to sit in that empty chair. If he does not, don't take the rejection personally you are probably too good for this guy.
- Tilting your head, touch your exposed neck and remember to smile.
- Ask this guy for help with something like, "What do you recommend drinking or eating on a day like this?" If he is a gentleman, he will take some time to explain.
- The other way is to drop something in front of him and walk away. This

was used even in the yesteryear; the old school way and it still works today.

Get a friend to practice these with you to polish up your confidence. Maybe you might feel that you are being too forward, but all you are doing is speeding up the process for finding love. Remember, wherever you are and go, smile, smile and smile more. After making all these gestures or movements to attract that guy in your radius, it might not work right away, on your first attempt. Don't lose heart, keep trying. Have fun with this process and enjoy yourself.

In closing this chapter, I am going to leave you with a tool that will help you to remember what you need to do when you are out in the world called **SOFTEN**. I learned this from Gregg Michaelsen.

- **S** is for smiling at him accompanied by that 5-second eye contact. It might take a few smiles to get his attention.
- **O** is an open body language. This includes you looking up and not looking down. Don't sit with your arms folded. It seems like closing yourself away from other people. You can cross your legs. This will make you look classy and confident.
- **F** is for leaning forward when talking to him. It shows that you are interested in the person you are talking to. Don't lean in too close like you are trying to throw in a kiss, no. Make sure you are facing the person in front of you. Some women have this habit of sitting with their side facing the guy. Even if you turn your face and look at him, it still shows that you are turning your energy away from this man in front of you. So, you must turn your whole body and face him. I was guilty of this once too.
- **T** is for touch. It's just a light and a brief touch on his arm or arm during a conversation. You can also do this while reaching for something that's close to him. Please don't knock his drink or plate over.
- **E** the eye contacts again. This is now the chance to gaze into his baby eyes and hold the gaze for a few seconds and move your gaze away from

him slowly. That will certainly make him want to come over and talk to you. When you do this more often it will become second nature.

- **N** is for nodding as he is talking to you, just to indicate you are paying attention, even if you want to run for the door.

So now you are all ready and prepared to get into the dating scene again. You know what relationship you are looking for and how to expedite the dating process, it's time to know how to date without losing yourself in the dating process.

17

DATING SMART

Dating smart is about the best ways to search for love without losing yourself in the dating process. The dating process keeps changing every day, and so do the people. Having an open mind and not expecting too much from the first dates is key to successful dating. If you go into dating with high expectations of meeting this perfect guy on a high horse and wearing shining armor, then you will be disappointed. This chapter will highlight what you need to know in order to determine whether the guy is good for you or not.

How to become a love magnet is also the other focus of this chapter, as it will teach you the tricks to be the best you can be to attract the right guy for you. Most of us women, get lost in the words that are said to us. These men sometimes are good at telling women what they want to hear. The trick is, do their words match their actions or not? If he promises to call or text you at a certain time, does he keep his word? Do you end up sending him a text to find out what happened to the text or call that he promised to send or call?

One other thing to highlight is not to trust your feelings too much. Your feelings are like your emotions, they go up and down, like your hormones. Your feelings also go hand in hand with your mood. Say for example if you don't feel like going to work, can you call your boss and tell him or her that you don't feel like coming to work that day? This is a recipe to get yourself fired from that job! So, the same applies to a relationship, our feelings can deceive us.

When you date smart, you keep things in perspective. Don't lose yourself in the dating process by making this process the center of your life. Make sure you still enjoy your life, your job, your family and take care of yourself. This will keep your life balanced and it will make you into a more interesting person to be around when you finally meet that special guy.

You see all the red flags as soon as they start flagging you down. Don't take it for granted that a person will change. That never happens, so don't expect this to happen for you. Never go for a date expecting to meet your match. Have an open mind and use this to meet new interesting people. Enjoy this process while you can, before building a genuine connection with your match.

You handle rejection with grace when you understand how to date smart. You are not a match for everyone. The fact that he dumped you does not mean that you will not find your match, you will. He is just not it. Rejection is inevitable in dating. So, don't spend too much time wallowing over it. Learn from it and use that as an experience. Dealing with rejection in a healthy way will increase your strength and resilience in your daily life. Don't suppress your feelings, acknowledge the hurt and disappointment and move on. Dwelling on it will not reverse the rejection, it will just add more pressure and frustration to your life.

Building boundaries is also another way of dating smart. Building healthy boundaries will protect you against being ill-treated by people around you including this new guy coming into your life. People will know how you will want to be treated once they know your boundaries. If these boundaries are crossed, then there will be consequences. A good example is when a guy is trying to sleep with you too soon and against your will. You make it clear that you are not interested, and he persists, then he should know that there will be consequences. A confident woman who dates smart will show this guy the door and not succumb to his pressure.

Don't be used by this new guy

This might be hard to spot for you at the beginning. Maybe on the second or third date, it might start to surface. I call these guys, "**leaches,**" because they can latch on you and suck the life out of you. Gregg Michaelsen calls them "*wet kittens.*" Send them to the shelter where they belong.

Signs to Watch Out For:

- He always has an excuse for leaving his wallet behind and relies on your money. He cannot support himself financially. Even if he was laid off work, if he cares for you, he will not ask for money from you. He will look for alternative means to support himself or get another job or a loan.
- He is very proud of what you have and shows it off to his friends. It means he is elevating his status and his ego and has no fear of appreciating what you have. His friends will put him on a pedestal because he was able to catch a big fish like you!
- He forgets your birthday, or any special occasions you value, but expects you to remember his. He will seem conveniently busy or unavailable, so he does not have to cough out his money for you.
- He calls you only when he wants to vent about something, he is frustrated, depressed, or horny. He has no time to call you and have a good conversation about your relationship or the date you had the other day. He might have some emotional and unhealthy mental issues that you are not aware of and he is using you for his emotional supports. He is a user, let him go and move on.

Listen to your gut feeling to know if you are being used.

The red flags

- Forgets Your Name.

How many ladies is this guy seeing that he does not remember who is who? This is the thing he should keep at the tip of his tongue, your name. It's about respect ladies and gentlemen. I can understand if he has a hard time pronouncing the name, but to have no clue who is standing in front of him is unacceptable.

- His Job/Career

His job title is not found on google! What does this guy do? He is probably a couch surfer and unemployed. I'm sure that is not what you are looking for. It's not that you are after his money, but he must have a genuine source of income. If he continues to avoid the question then, it's time for you to go home for the night.

- The "L" Bomb

Before the first date is over, he is already madly in love with you. He confesses how much you mean to him. Like dude, I just met you and you have no idea what I am made of. It's preferable to meet and get to know each other. You can say well there is love at first sight. Yes, there is a thing like that, but it does not happen all the time. Just be cautious. What's the rush?

- His Outfit

Is his wardrobe malfunctioning? His clothes are not clean and look visibly wrinkled! The first date is to impress you and if he cannot take the time to give you that, then I have doubts if he will ever step up his game. It's easy for the guys than it is for women. A pair of clean jeans, clean or polished shoes and a clean t-shirt and he is good to go.

- Dirty Syndrome

If your date appears for the date with dirty fingernails, uncombed hair and looks on the rough edges. He smells like a box of cigarettes and alcohol is on his breath. Do yourself a favor and say goodbye. You don't need that in your life. You are not his addiction and grooming counselor.

- Addicted to his phone

He cannot finish a sentence talking to you and his phone is ringing or messages are coming in. If he is expecting a very important call, then he should advise you beforehand that he will need to be excused to get that call. It's called respect! You are not going to be with him for the rest of the night. If he is glued to his phone, then he is probably not interested in you as he cannot focus on what is in front of him. Phones should be put away, so you have time to look into each other's eyes and see if there is chemistry between the two of you.

- He brags about his assets and bank accounts

You are not a gold digger. You are a woman of value and you can hold your own. He is insecure in some ways. He is overcompensating for something, so you get blinded by that? What is this dude hiding? You can gently tell him that it's too early to know all that personal details about him and see if he will get the hint. If not, then it's up to you to put up with that childish behavior.

- His head is swaying around looking at other women

I know men are visual animals, but if this guy misses his mouth while eating because he is looking at another gorgeous, Lady with a big butt and a pair of Dolly Parton boobs, then that's what he wants not you. Men can look, but if you catch him several times drooling over other women, you need to have a conversation with him or just go to the washroom and never come back to the table. Head back home, take a long bath, not forgetting the soft music and candles around the bathtub. It's called self-care and self-love

Become A Love Magnet

Becoming a love magnet is a process of discovering and maintaining who you truly are. It's about shifting your attention to what you love about yourself and what you would love to attract in the partner you intend to marry. The Law of Attraction is all about positive energy from the universe to you. This will require you to feel, think in alignment with your goals of meeting that special person that will rock your world. To manifest this wonderful person, you need to start feeling great about the fact that you are deserving of a terrific partner, who will treat you as an equal. Being a love magnet also involves shifting yourself to be the partner you wish to marry. You will know who you are as a partner, look at how satisfied you are with your life and how clear you are about what kind of romantic relationship you want to be in.

A love magnet does not cry over a guy. Don't cry yourself to sleep if he does not call you within the time you expect him to call. He might not call at all. Don't give him your power by allowing you to feel bad or not good enough for him. Don't send him a text begging for an explanation of what you did wrong on the date. If there is something you did wrong, he should be man enough to tell you. If he does not, then don't hold yourself hostage to things that you don't know. This is an assumption that you are making for yourself to justify your insecurities. It might be on your first date and this happens. If you don't work on your self-esteem, self-love, self-confidence, or have no idea who you are and what you are worth, then you will continue to meet the same jerks with different names, different shapes, and sizes.

Identify Your Deal Breakers

These are the things that you cannot settle for.

- Are you looking for marriage with or without kids? Do you still want to be a mum again? How about pets?

- Is it the height and weight of an individual that puts you off?

- Are you okay with a person who smokes while you don't? Does he smoke in his car or in his house? He might say he will quit but, I am sure you have heard that before. If you don't smoke are you okay with the risks of second-hand smoking? So, don't date a guy with his potential to quit smoking, that's a deal-breaker.

- Do you mind getting together with a person who is paid less than you and are you ok to be the bigger breadwinner in the marriage/relationship or not? Are you comfortable with his career and is he okay with what you do for a living?

- Does distance matter for you? Do, you just want to date people from your community? What are you willing to compromise in this new relationship?

- How is his personal hygiene? Is that a turn off to you? Can you put up with his smelly armpits and smelly feet?

- A guy who is full of himself? This is the type of man who talks about no one else but himself?

- A guy who has verbal diarrhea about his ex or late wife? This will take time away for him to get to know you. It also shows he has not healed or is still very bitter or in love with the previous person.

- He has a posse that is always around him. It means you don't get some quality time with him without his friends showing up uninvited. More is not merrier if you are honestly trying to get to know this guy. If this is happening, then he is friend-zoning you. You might want to have a conversation with him if you really like him.

- He is a loner. Having friends is healthy as it will give you time alone when he is with his buddies. If he is a loner, he can be clingy and needy. This kind of man can be boring as he is used to being on his own and having you around might be too much for him. He might not want you to have friends as well.

- The way he communicates with other people, is he respectful? Does he treat restaurant staff with respect? The way he treats that server in the restaurant is the way he will treat you one day. It's called the "waitress test."

- What's your take on a guy who has never left college days? This is the guy that gets hammered on a date with you. Do you want to be the one calling a taxi for him to go home?

- Run for the hills if he does not pick up the bill for the first date. It means he is stingy with his money and might have issues later to take you out for dates without asking you to pay for yourself. A gentleman will pick up the tab on the first date and on all the dates. You as an independent woman will also offer to pay as well, and a gentleman will decline the offer and pay for the bill. When a guy pays for the bill it makes a woman feel valued and appreciated.

- A guy who is very pushy about getting between the sheets with you before you are ready for it. He makes a condition to continue with the relationship. Red flag. Run from that man without values. You should not be forced to do anything that you are not ready to do. Some guys might start to grope you inappropriately and in a nonconsensual way on the first date. That's so disrespectful. Beware of perverts.

Don't Be Too Aloof

Do not try to be Miss perfect. No one is perfect. You play hard to get and don't express your interest. When the guy calls, you don't even express your excitement that he called. When he pays the bills after having a meal, you don't even show your appreciation. Sitting with your arms crossed in front of this guy shows that you can't wait to get out of there, away from this guy with this kind of body language. This will keep you in the singles lane forever, unless if you change your attitude and behavior.

Playing Games

Not being your authentic self. You pretend to be someone you are not and giving all these lame excuses why you are not available to go on a date. If you want to play hard to get, then do it at your own risk. It does not mean that you should fall in love with a guy after the first date. You just need to indicate your interest and the rest will follow if the guy is interested.

You respond to his messages with one-word answers when he has sent you a whole paragraph.

You might give the guy a wrong name and then he discovers that it was not your right name, that's embarrassing. How do you explain that?

Don't Make The Guy Your Hobby

The guy will call you last minute to hang out, and you cancel your plans with yourself or family just to go out with him. This shows that you have no life of your own. You are just waiting for his call to get something to do. Get busy with your own life, that way you don't end up idle at home and being his option.

To know that you are making him your hobby you will be doing the following:

- Obsessed about his whereabouts daily and who he is with.
- Overly doting him he feels suffocated.
- Poking your nose in his business trying to know too much too soon.
- Getting too possessive, too clingy and needy. As a result, you will start complaining about him not spending enough time with you.
- Stripping him off his alone time with his caveman mates and nagging him about not caring about you.

This will spook him and chase him away so fast he will not want to see you again! Make sure to have your own hobbies that will keep you busy and out of his hair all the time. You will remain mysterious and very interesting. This will create more curiosity in his mind about what else is going to hit. When you have hobbies, these can be a source of memorable moments when you decide to spend time together doing what you love. Memories usually keep the relationship alive and add meaning to it. Many people have created long term relationships because of the memories that they have shared. I know for me happy memories have helped to heal and create better friendships with my loved ones.

Don't put the guy on a pedestal. You treat him like he is the most perfect creation under the sun. No one is perfect. All you need is treat him with respect and that is the best gift you can give a man. Just accept him for who he is, and he will do the same. He also needs to know that you are normal and can live with his imperfections. Don't chase him, I cannot say this enough. If this guy really wants to know you, he will put in the work to know you.

After the first date, you can send a message to thank him for the date and the time you spent together. Don't ask him when he will call you again! That is not your place. If you do this you are showing your masculine energy instead of taking a step back into your feminine energy. Men are hunters, so let him hunt you down.

- You feel entitled

Because the guy has money does not make you entitled to get expensive gifts and flowers every time he comes to see you. Just draw this guy in with gratitude and the rest will follow. Let him offer to do things for you. Don't demand. This is a love repellent.

- Masculine Behavior

This is very common to some women who have been single for too long. They feel the guy cannot do or perform certain tasks well, like loading the dishwasher. You ask him to help you with the dishes and then you are over his shoulders trying to show him how to do it when he has not asked for your help. Leave it up to him and when he can't load it well, he will figure it out himself. Don't be his mother! When you are driving somewhere, you are always trying to give him directions when he knows how to get there. Give him a break!

Instead, if you want to help, then ask him if you can help, otherwise, let him figure it out himself.

• Instant Relationship

Do not fall into the trap of trying too hard to make a guy like you. You treat him like your boyfriend or husband on the second date, really? You must take some time to know this guy and like him. Men like to feel like they got chosen from the millions of guys you are dating. This will push him away as you will seem like you are desperate for a relationship. Take your sweet and sexy time to know this guy and vice versa.

• Don't do Cybersex

Don't fall victim to cybersex. Some men just want cybersex and nothing more. To be proactive, don't flirt too much or do any suggestive flirting through instant messages or emails until you have met in person. Sometimes they will tell you they have a connection with you after the first week of communication. They will also tell you how lonely they are and how they really want a woman like you in their lives. They will start asking some suggestive questions and before you know it you are sucked up into the cybersex relationship. So, just be on the lookout for perverts like these as they are not looking for meaningful relationships, but just to satisfy their devoid lives.

First Date Dos and Don'ts

It does not matter where you have met this new guy. For the first date, try to meet in a public place. The place does not have to be fancy or formal. A formal place is at a restaurant. The informal place could be a bowling place, golf, or drink at a bar. It must be a place where you, the woman does not have to drive more than 45 minutes to get to the date. He must come to where you are, not the other way around. If he invites you over to his house, don't go. You don't know this guy at all and already he is inviting you to his house. What if he is a serial killer or rapist on the lose? It's not wise for the woman to drive that far for a first date. It must be a place that you are familiar with. Maybe later in the dating process. Remember you are the prize in this dating process, so you don't have to go out of your way to meet this man.

Do not agree to go on a date with a guy you meet online or anywhere without talking to him on the phone. Talking to him on the phone will give you that extra chance to check if there is an attraction or connection. If you like him over the phone, there is a fifty-fifty chance that there will be some chemistry when you meet on the date. If he is boring over the phone that might be a sign you will not like him in person. Some people never improve in person just saying!

This is a chance for you to know if he has verbal diarrhea or not. Nonstop talkers might not give you a chance to put in your words. If you really like him, put your hand gently on top of his and say, "Is there anything you would like to know about me?" If he does not get the hint, then it's time to find the nearest exit and head home.

Do not bring your ex or late spouse on the date with you. Talking too much about your late spouse or your ex on a date is a big red flag. It means a lot of things. For example, you are still in love with your ex, you have not healed from his passing. Or you are still bitter about what happened in your last relationship. It might also indicate that you hold grudges and don't forgive easily. So, don't start running your mouth about your previous relationship. Be mindful.

What Not to Ask on The First Date

Remember the first date is a date to meet and see if there is any chemistry and you visualize them in your life. This is a chance for you to see if there are three things that you like about this man in front of you. It's not an interrogation date where you want to squeeze out so much information from this poor guy. Take it is easy on him and give him a chance to show you who he is. Ask open-ended questions that will make him feel comfortable, e.g. "Tell me about your best vacation spot that you have been to recently and why?" You can also talk about your jobs, hobbies, movies and places you have visited.

Here are questions not to ask on your first date:

1. Why are you still single? This is not very appropriate as you are just, as single too. He might not feel comfortable to answer especially if he was to blame for the relationship break down. He might also take it the wrong way and think that there is something wrong with him being single. You might ask, how long have you been single? This is much better as you will know if he is dateable material or not. If he has just gotten out of a relationship last month then, he might not be ready to date yet. If he has been off the dating scene for more than 10 years after his divorce or bereavement, you might want to think twice about going ahead with this one. I know this is one question everyone gets tempted to ask on the first date. Save it for later in the dating process.

2. Why did your last relationship end? As much as you want to know why he broke up with his ex, he might throw it back at you to answer the same question. Let him tell you if he wants to. The first date is just to see who this guy is and if there is any chemistry. You are not the FBI to get information out of this new guy. This might open a can of worms with some people, as they will get a chance to complain about their exes on the first date, which I'm sure you are not ready for. I know when you have lost a spouse when someone asks you what happened to your

last relationship and you will say that they are deceased. You should see their eyeballs falling to the floor in utter shame. Most of the time it's followed by a huge apology. One time I asked this question to a guy and he said, "My relationship ended because I wanted to meet you." So, after this, what will you say for yourself?

3. Where are you really from? This is a stinker to most people of color. They feel like they don't belong to that country where they are in. It feels like a very derogatory question and a bit segregated. Even if you are curious to know where they were born, save that for another date. You might say, "So did you grow up in this part of the city?" This more general because even the locals might not have grown up in the same city.

4. When was the last time you had sex? Or how many people did you have sex with? This is none of anyone's business. This is sensitive information. This will make the other person very uncomfortable and might cause them to shut down for the rest of the date, or even leave. Your date will feel judged and put on the spot. If you want to date a saint, then go to the convent or to heaven. Here on earth none is perfect including you. You will be lucky if you get an answer to this question. You might get a free shower of his drink or a third finger waved at you. Don't ask anything sexual on the first date at all. If they ask you this question, just politely tell them that it's too intrusive and none of their business. You leave with your head held up high.

5. Where do you see this relationship heading? You are not in a relationship yet! You just met this guy. This is very premature as you barely know this guy. If you assume that he likes you and wants to date you, by the way, he is treating you on this date then you are setting yourself up for heartbreak. You will come off as needy and desperate for a relationship. This is a big red flag to the guy as it might portray instant relationship status from your part. Calm down, slow down and take baby steps.

6. How much do you make? Red flag, you are a gold digger! Asking someone to reveal their income on the first date is a big no, no. This is

will depict you as an opportunist and materialist. Asking this question will come off as you being only interested in what you get out of the relationship financially. Your intentions are a bit sketchy, to be honest. You will seem like you are more interested in his wallet than him as a human being. Even if this is not your intention it will come out that way.

7. What Is Your Most Embarrassing Moment? No one wants to start blushing about their embarrassing moments on their first date. This is oversharing of information on the first date. Ask the opposite of this question. "What is your most memorable event?" Same applies to you, don't overshare information about your life. It's a turn-off.

9 Talking about marriage, wedding and having children. You might come off as being very desperate for a relationship. This is a pushy and sensitive subject and will scare the guy away. You don't even know if he is right for you yet and already you are planning a wedding with this guy? Give him a break and pump up your brakes and know this guy first.

Now that you how to date smart, you can recognize the red flags and know when a guy is using you, it is time for you to find out if you have melted his heart.

18

SIGNS THAT HE IS INTO YOU

1. He becomes stupid and awkward around you. He might start choking on his words or he starts to stammer. Yet, when you spoke to him on the phone, he did not stammer at all. If you ask him something, he is slow to respond, while at the same time he is just awed by your beauty. Let him breathe and give him a chance to collect himself.

2. He laughs at your jokes and he thinks you are a standup comedian. He might just be giggling at everything and anything you do. He is nervously trying so hard to impress you. He is smiling constantly. He laughs at your goofiness.

3. He Makes Eye Contact. He can't stop staring at you. His pupils dilate and he appears like this big eye balled baby.

4. He Starts Mirroring You. He will start talking like you, he might lean in when you lean in as well. When you sit back into your chair, he does the same thing. You smile, he smiles. This can happen to you too if you like a guy, you start to mirror his actions. It shows that you're smitten with them and trying to belong to their world.

5. He changes his schedule for you. He will change his life schedule to be able to meet with you, not the other way around. A gentleman always wants to put his right foot forward. So changing his schedule will indicate how important you are to him. He is the chaser, so he will do

anything to meet you.

6. He walks close to the street so he can protect you. When a guy cares he will make sure the walks close to the street so that he protects you from the crazy drivers on the roads. He will also slow down his pace to walk alongside you.

7. He makes you feel comfortable, to be yourself, you don't have to change your behavior when he is around you. He loves you with your crazies. You are comfortable with him with and without makeup, with your bad morning breath and on bad hair days. He accepts your goofy selfies and he will never have enough of them. He will send you his goofy pictures too.

8. He loves to learn more and everything about you. He will listen to you talking without brushing you off and talking over you. He will pay attention to every important detail about you.

9. He grounds you. You just feel this sense of safety around him and he will feel the same too if there is a connection between the two of you. You know you can trust this man with your fears, insecurities and even your heart.

10. He keeps his word. If he says he will call you he will call. If he says he will show up at a certain time he will do so. If he promises to help you with anything, he will do so under no duress at all.

19

CONCLUSION

I n conclusion, let's just go through the pointers to keep at your fingertips as you begin your new journey. Being humans, you might still have some questions lingering at the back of your minds. The big questions are, where do you begin, where do you stop, and will this work for you? All that I can say is, you never know if this information will work for you until you try it out. It might take you some time to go through the healing process, that's ok if you put your mind to it and give yourself consent to heal. You will surprise yourself and heal.

You have wallowed in your pain long enough and have bonded with your *Widowhood* baggage and nothing has eased your pain. The pain is still there and it's getting worse. Don't get stuck in that zone. It's not healthy for you and everyone around you. Getting stuck in your *Widowhood* baggage will get you to bleed on everyone. Good thing, now you know how to love yourself and practice self-care. Negativity should be kept out of your life, as that will keep you bonded to your *Widowhood* baggage.

Positive self-talk helps your healing journey by attracting positive energy to your life moving forward. The Law of Attraction works for you in a positive environment, so keep that in mind. You cannot share love when your cup is empty, let your cup overflow first, then you can share what is overflowing.

You have done part of the healing and transformation journey already by purchasing this book to prepare you. it might seem insurmountable, but now you, know how to deal with those self-limiting thoughts. Healing and forgiveness work hand in hand. You cannot truly heal when you are still holding onto unforgiveness. Forgiveness will let you release the pain and healing begins. Keeping that laundry list of all those hurts and the people who caused you pain will weigh you down. Forgiveness starts with you that is the key, to a successful healing process. You can skip your meal, but do not skip your healing process.

You never applied to be a widow but crying about it is not going to change it, unless you take action to change your situation. There is a time for everything a time to mourn, to grieve, to heal and celebrate the legacy of your late spouse. Don't let the death of your spouse claim another life, YOU.

For the divorcees, this will allow you to move on and not look back thinking you wasted your time with that dude who dumped you. At least I am sure you have learned something from that experience.

Regretting that you were married to that loser will not turn back the clock. This is your time to look after yourself, love yourself and transfer the regret to him.

Don't let the naysayers tell you that they have tried to heal and find happiness, it did not work. Remember to smile and walk away with your heart and dignity in one place. You are not them and you will never be. These people have no idea what you have gone through and who you truly are. The only person who knows you it's you. You can be happy and find love again.

If you plan to get back into the dating scene, remember to be true to yourself about what relationships you are looking for. Your kids should be on board so they can help and support you. Go easy on them, as they might still feel that you are trying to replace their dad. Going back into the dating scene, if you still feel like you are cheating on your late husband, it means you are not ready to date. You still need more time to heal and deal with your emotions.

Continue to work on your self-confidence, self-worth, self-awareness, self-esteem and create healthy boundaries for yourself. Remember you are a woman of value; the grieving process might have eroded that part of you, but you can get that back. Shift your mindset from the "poor me" and "why me?" mindset, to "what can I do?" mindset. To move on in life and be a better version of yourself.

I WISH YOU THE BEST IN YOUR NEW JOURNEY IN LIFE.
MUCH LOVE,
ROSEMARY TRISH MUPAMBWA.

RECOMMENDED RESOURCES

Understanding Different Types of Men and How to Date Them-By Gregg Michaelsen. (24 January 2019.)

Middle Aged and Kickin" It- A Woman's Guide to Dating over 40, 50 and Beyond-By Gregg Michaelsen. (4 January 2019).

Night Movies- The Science of Making Him Fall in Love with You-By Gregg Michealsen. (24 January 2019).

The Man God Has for You-7 Traits to Help You Determine Your Life Partner -By Stephan Labossiere. (January 2018).

He's Lying Sis-Uncover the Truth Behind His Words and Actions- By Stephan Labossiere. (20 April 2019)

He Is History You Are Not-Surviving Divorce After 40-Erica Manfred Foreword by Tina B. Tessina, PhD (2009).

How to Get A Man Getting Played: 29 Dating Secrets to Catch Me Right, Set Your Standards, and Eliminate Time Wasters-By Bruce Bryns (8 January 2019).

Live Like You Are Dying- 20 Steps to Awaken Your Genius- By Gregg Michaelsen.

(24 January 2019).

Finding Love After Heartbreak Vol 1- By Stephan Labossiere. (24 April 2019).

Successful Dating and Relationships After Divorce- By Toby Hazlewood. (30 December 2018).

He's Gone Now What? - How to Get Over the Break-Up and Prepare to Love Again- By Gregg Michaelsen (15 January 2019).

Supercharge Your Love Life -14 Game-Changers to Change Your Life – By Gregg Michaelsen (2017).

How to age Gracefully -Growing older with grace - Elan & Style -By Kristi Belle (2008)

Why so many of us get stuck in toxic relationships -By Mitzi Bockmann (2018).

Owning your emotional Baggage in Relationships- By Robin Hoffman, contributor Health Coach. (October 19, 2013)

10 Dating Tips for Widows Nearing (And Over) 50 -By Sabra Robinson (July 8, 2017)

Don't Let Him Use You-Either He Wants to Date You or He Can GTFO -Tough Love -By Jennifer Lee

Are You Getting What You Deserve? 11 Ways You Might Be Settling Without Even Realizing It -Tough Love -Aya Tsintziras

Non-Negotiable Rules for Dating Smart In 2018 – by Elizabeth Overstreet. (February 5th 2018.)

8 Qualities I Thought I Wanted in A Partner Until I Met My Current Boyfriend -by Kerry Carmody

Dating from Inside Out: How to Use the Law of Attraction in Matters of The Heart -By Dr Paulette Kouffman Sherman (February 2008).

A Guide to Getting Back in The Dating Game After A Long Dry Spell- By Kate Ferguson.

Types of Baggage That Ruin Relationships- By Lisa Duffy (May 12, 2016)

8 Types of Romantic Relationships Everyone Should Know About – By Lindsay Geller (May 30, 2018).

Types of guys you "Almost" Date- By Jennifer Lee

10 Questions You Should Never Ask on A First Date – By Kelsey Borresen, HuffPost. US

https://the30club.wordpress.com/ 2008/ 12/ 09/ 8-different-personality-types-of-men/

How to Start Dating Again After Ending A Long-Term Relationship-By Dani-Elle Dube.

Does He Want an Open Relationship? 11 Signs He Wants to See Other People – By Giulia Simolo. (2019).

Fix What's Wrong – by Sally B. Watkins, MSW

Ways Smart, Savvy, Empowered Women Date Very-By Kristina Marchant

How to Be A Confident Dater - By Carly Spindel. (July 6th, 2018)

Types of Men A Woman Can Meet in Her Lifetime-By Dayan Masinde (March 28th, 2017)

9 Qualities That Show He Is Definitely in The One. Number 7 Is A Must - By Afrizap (January 2015.)

How to Date Without Losing Yourself-By Michelle Farris.

8 Ways to Stop Self-Sabotaging Your Dates - And Get A Great Guy - By Michelle Lewis (August 3, 2015)

15 First Date Red Flags That Scream -No Second Date! - By Mackenzie Johnson- (July 22, 2015)

Why It's Time to Ditch Guys and Date Dating Yourself- By Franki Hanke.

The Power to Heal Is Within You- by Louise L. Hay (1991).

The Healing Handbook - A Beginner's Guide and Journal to Meditation – By Jodi Levy. (1999).

How to Start Loving Yourself – By Tanaaz (2019).

Self-Esteem, Self-Acceptance, or Self-Love-What's the Difference? - By Darlene Lancer JD MFT. (2011)

How to Get Better Sleep – By Melinda Smith, M.A., Lawrence Robinson, Robert Segal, M.A. Last (June 2019).

Examples of Positive and Negative Automatic Thoughts – By Rick Ingram and Kathy Wisnicki (1988).

What Is Gratitude and Why It Is So Important – By Ralph Waldo Emerson. (February 02 2017).

https://www.revolutionarylifestyledesign.com/reframe-negative-thoughts/

How to Stop Worrying – By Help Guide.Org (2019)

Steps to End Chronic Worrying – By Denise Mann. (2019)

Harm Reduction on Yourself – By Denise Lambert. (2019)

https://www.whatsyourgrief.com/don't-know-anymore-loss-grief-loss-identity/

Who Are You? – By Hay House (Energy Healing Made Easy Online Video Course) (2019)

Benefits We Can Reap from The Power of Visualization Immediately -By Jenna McNaney, Contributor. (February 12th, 2015).

Get What You Want Through Visualization –By the College of Metaphysical Studies (2019).

How to Forgive Someone Who Has Hurt You: Even When Forgiveness Feels Impossible: by Dr Wayne W. Dyer (2019).

You Can Be Happy No Matter What – Five Principles for Keeping Life in Perspective – By Richard Carlson, PhD (1997).

Online Dating Success Secrets for Women 40/50+ - How to Find True Lasting Love-Attract Your Love Hero/Like I did -By Caryl Westmore (2017).

Is your emotional baggage holding you back – By Brianna Steinhilber (July 24, 2018).

Reduce Stress and Improve Your Life with Positive Talk- Develop the Positive Self-Habit! - By Elizabeth Scott, MS (November 23, 2018).

WIDOWHOOD

Avoid These Mistakes When Working with Widows – By Barbara Shapiro (June 13, 2017).

10 Things I Wish Someone Had Told Me About Becoming A Widow – By Stacy Feintuch (May 25, 2017).

Looking for Love Again: A Widows Guide – By Sienna Jae Fein, Contributor (December 6, 2017)

Learning More About Working with Widows – By Olivia Mellan (February 24, 2014)

Widow to Widow: Thoughtful Practical Ideas for Rebuilding Your Life-By Genevieve Davis Ginsburg, M.S. (1997).

https://www.huffpost.com/entry/widowhood_b_3648836 (December 6, 2017)

Loss Is A Four-Letter Word-A Bereavement Boot Camp for The Widowed-Kick Grief in The Ass and Take Your Life Back -By Carole Brody Fleet (2018).

Growing Through Divorce – By Jim Smoke. (Foreword Robert Schuller) (1978).

Divorced & Scared No More- Dating After Divorce from Lemons to Zesty Lemon Sorbet -By Tasher Tony Haynes (2016).

10 ways to stand as a widow – By Herb Scribner (September 10, 2014)

Moving Forward on Your Own-A Financial Guide for Widows- By Kathleen M. REHL, PhD CFD (2018)

Healing A Spouses Grieving Heart-100 Practical Ideas After Your Husband or Wife Dies-Compassionate Advice and Simple Activities for Widows and Widowers -By Alan D. Wolfelt, PhD (2003)

Change Your Mindset, Not Your Man- Learn to Love What's Right Instead of Trying to

Post-Widowhood: Reinventing Your Future - By Jod Kirsch, CFP (July 24, 2018).

Widow, 32, Opens Up on Finding Love After Husband's Death- By Shari Sputerman (October 10, 2017).

Widowhood Practices: The lmo Experience, by Owerri, Multi-Purpose Hall, Mimeographed -by Nzewi, E.N. (June 6, 1989).

Widowhood Practices: Female Prejudice, -by Owerri, Multi-Purpose Hall, (6 June 1989).

The King in *Every Man* - London: University Press- (1972), by Eze, O.C. and O.E. Nwebo.

Widowhood Practices: Law and Custom- by Owerri, Multi-Purpose Hall, (Mimeographed).

Widowhood Practices in Africa: A Preliminary Survey and Analysis- by Owerri, Multi-purpose Hall, (6 June 1989) (Mimeographed), Stringfellow, William.

*After Losing the Love of My Life, I'm Dating for The First Time in Decades-*By Jim Walter (September 25, 2018).

The Joy of Mourning: On Grief and of Resurrection, by Sojourner.

India's Widows, Abused at Home, Have Sought Refuge in This Holy City for Centuries, India Dispatch, By Kai Schultz, (August 27, 2019).

Widows Wear Stilettos -A Practical and Emotional Guide for The Young

Widow-By Carole Brody Fleet with Syd Harriet, PhD., Psy.D. (2009).

About the Author

Rosemary Trish Mupambwa, a mother of three, and an author, was a fashion model, former college lecturer in Zimbabwe, and a Salvation Army Corps Secretary for 11 years. She was also a League of Mercy Secretary for the Salvation Army in Zimbabwe.

She went to college in the United Kingdom and obtained a Diploma in College Education. She moved to Canada in 2006, got a Diploma in Social Work, a Diploma in Business Administration, and a Degree in Sociology from Athabasca University in Canada. She has been a Domestic Violence Counsellor for 11 years and has worked in the Mental Health field for 12 years. Rosemary is also an Internationally Certified Relationship/Dating Expert. She is a qualified Transformation and Life Strategist. She runs a meet up group for singles in Calgary. She is a Commissioner of Oaths with Alberta Health Services.

Rosemary is a Certified public speaker through the Mega Speakers by JT Foxx. She has been a Speaker with the Women's Talk Groups and has been an MC at several events in Calgary. Rosemary organizes a relationship workshop for couples and singles as well as a healing retreat organizer. Her work is the result of a lot of research which she has done on why relationships succeed and fail.

Being a widow herself, she has worked with widows, divorcees and other singles to get their power back instead of being stuck in their pain or grief.

Rosemary loves fashion, laughs a lot and is very passionate about bringing humor to people. Her big contagious smile is her signature, and humour is her trademark. She draws her strength from her faith, and her children Ruvimbo Natasha, Ronnie and Ropafadzo Tsitsi Mupambwa.

You can connect with me on:
- https://www.roseslifecoaching.com
- https://www.facebook.com/roseslifecoach
- https://www.facebook.com/Singleafterwidowhooddivorce
- https://www.instagram.com/rosemary.trish